Discove
and N

Already published:
Discovering Aberdeenshire
Discovering Angus & The Mearns
Discovering Argyll, Mull & Iona
Discovering the Black Isle
Discovering Cheshire
Discovering Coastal Lancashire
Discovering the Cotswolds
Discovering Cumbria
Discovering Dumfriesshire
Discovering East Lothian
Discovering Fife
Discovering Galloway
Discovering Inland Lancashire
Discovering Inverness-shire
Discovering Lewis and Harris
Discovering the Pentland Hills
Discovering Speyside
Discovering The Water of Leith
Discovering West Lothian
Discovering the Yorkshire Dales

Other books in the Discovering Series by Ron & Marlene Freethy are:
Discovering Cheshire
Discovering Cumbria
Discovering Coastal Lancashire
Discovering Inland Lancashire
Discovering The Yorkshire Dales

Discovering Exmoor and North Devon

RON & MARLENE FREETHY

JOHN DONALD PUBLISHERS LTD
EDINBURGH

John Donald Publishers Ltd,
138 St Stephen Street, Edinburgh EH3 5AA.

ISBN 0 85976 343 9

British Library Cataloguing-in-Publication Data.
A catalogue record for this book is available from the British Library.

Phototypeset by Newtext Composition Ltd, Glasgow.
Printed & bound in Great Britain by Scotprint Ltd, Musselburgh.

Contents

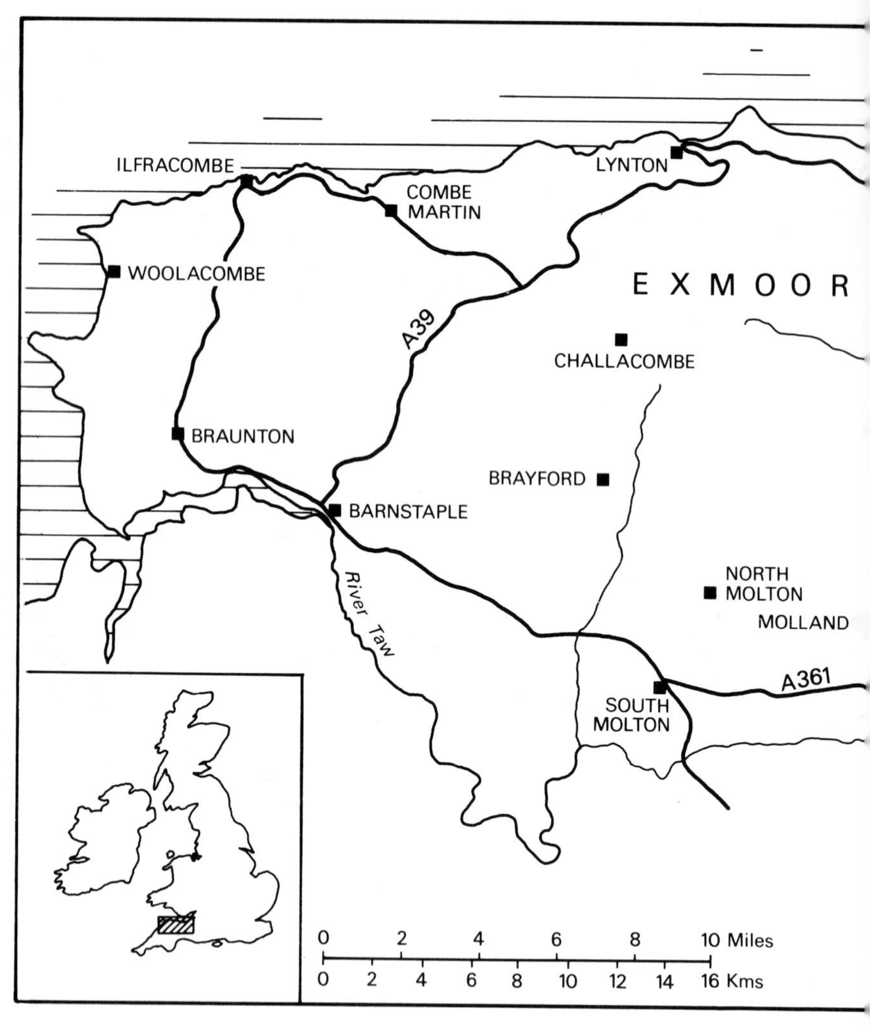

Location Map.

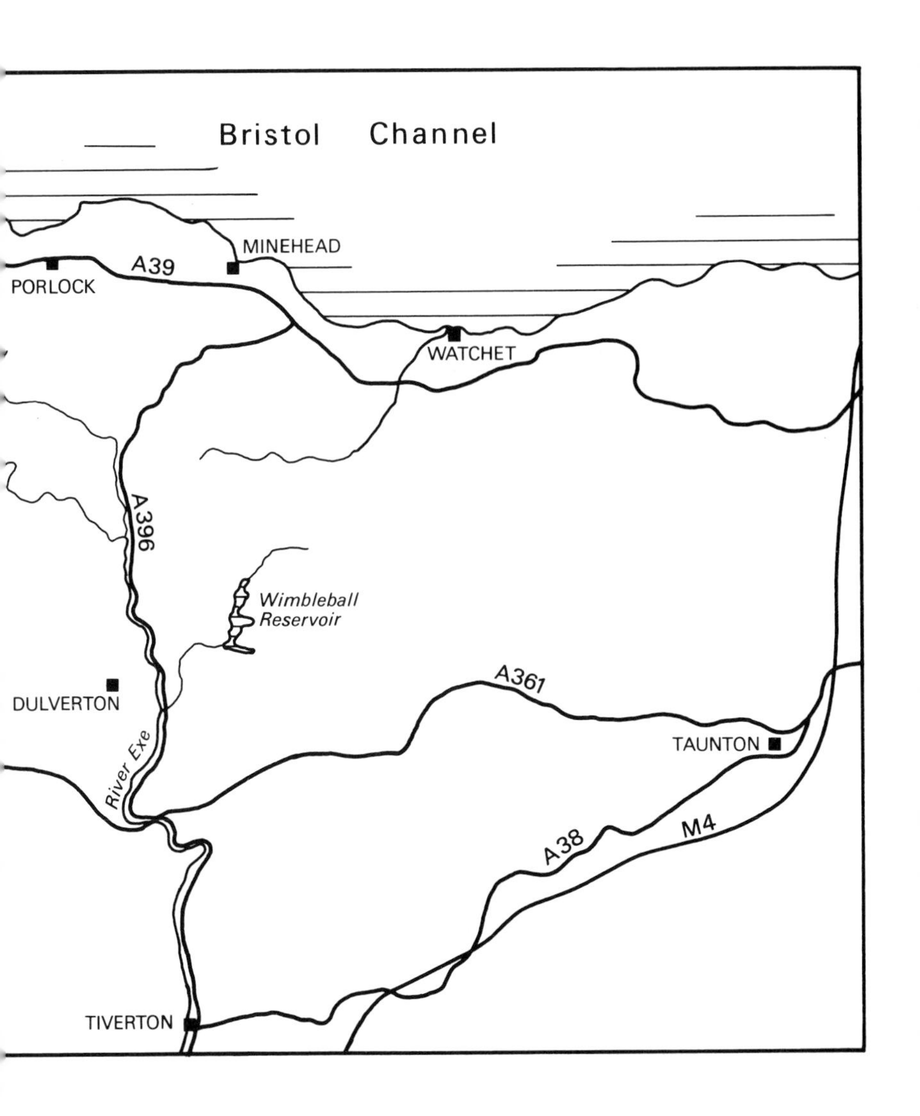
Bristol Channel
MINEHEAD
A39
PORLOCK
WATCHET
A396
Wimbleball
Reservoir
DULVERTON
River Exe
A361
TAUNTON
A38
M4
TIVERTON

Acknowledgements

When our friends and relatives, Bob and Sue Mahon, bought a hotel on the North Devon coast we knew that we loved the area but never dreamed that it would result in a book in the *Discovering* series. We were, and still are to some extent visitors, rather than residents around Exmoor but the situation is changing. It began with the discovery that the hotel was once the home of Sir Thomas Hewitt, a London lawyer who along with his friend George Newnes was instrumental in building the cliff railway and the Lynton to Barnstaple narrow-gauge railway. We spent parts of our summers guiding hotel visitors around the area, and during the winters we spent January at the hotel whilst our friends took a well-earned holiday. Thus our knowledge of the haunting area of Exmoor grew and we found local librarians and tourist information officers more than helpful. We noticed that there were many books about Exmoor, but all were more academic than this present work. We have written for visitors who want a background to the history, natural history, geology, archaeology and literature of Exmoor and the North Devon coast. We have also searched out the most exciting places to visit.

Whilst preparing the draft of this manuscript during early 1991 we were also working on a childrens' television series for the BBC and the result was that we made short films about Henry Williamson's *Tarka the Otter*, the cliff railway at Lynton and the quince honey farm at South Molton.

Introduction

No book is written without help and we are particularly grateful to the tourist information officers at Barnstaple, Tiverton and Minehead for keeping us supplied with information, and to the chef at the Hewitt's hotel for keeping us supplied with equally essential calories. To Bob and Susan Mahon we give our special thanks for a comfortable bed, good conversation and for the loan of a small white terrier as a companion for our own large black labrador.

CHAPTER 1

The Natural Exmoor

Exmoor became a National Park in 1954 and it is the smallest such area in Britain. It covers some 17,000 acres or 265 square miles, of which 188 are in Somerset with the remaining 77 in Devon. The National Park runs from Combe Martin in the west as far as Minehead in the east and includes some of the most dramatic coastline scenery in Britain. The boundary swings in a south-easterly direction curving around the Brendon Hills and then twists westwards around the south of Dulverton and Astey Common. The boundary circle is completed by returning to Combe Martin via Blackmoor Gate.

The centre of Exmoor was once a hunting forest, but the word forest did not have its modern meaning then, but was an area devoted to the preservation and hunting of beasts, especially deer which required shelter belts of trees and open areas in which to feed. The upland plateau is called the Chains which is an area of blanket bog on which grows the largest area of deer grass *Trichophorum cespitosum* to be found anywhere in southern England. The Chains are like a gigantic sponge and from it ooze thousands of streams or 'waters' as they are called locally and which explain why Exmoor has such an abundance of little bridges. These waters gradually merge into larger rivers such as the East and West Lyn, the Barle, the Mole and the Exe itself, which tumble down along precipitous combes. The northern waters eventually form the East and West Lyn Rivers which fall more than 1500 feet (457 m) within four miles and rush into Lynmouth. Normally the flat soft surface of the Chains can absorb heavy rainfall or snowmelt and release it gradually. This natural safety valve, however, failed on August 15th 1952, when after an horrendous storm a devastating wave of water struck Lynmouth (see Chapter 6).

Waters which flow from the southern end of the Chains are much less fierce and many of the small tributaries are captured by a dammed area called Pinkworthy Pond created by the Knight family. From Pinkworthy the Barle flows through Simonsbath,

Spring squill a feature of the coast of Devon.

Withypool and Tarr Steps before reaching Dulverton. The Exe also gathers its waters on the Chains and soon its valley deepens and its famous Cleve slices across the middle moor. The Exe flows through Exford, Winsford and Bridgeton and on to Dulverton near which the Barle and the Exe join. The Exe retains its name after the Barle has been swallowed and continues out of Exmoor via Exbridge and Tiverton before flowing through Exeter and on to the sea at Exmouth. The Mole absorbs the Crooked Oak River and then the Bray before itself merging into the Taw which reaches the sea at Barnstaple.

Apart from these river valleys Exmoor has extensive coastal heaths and slopes richly clothed in trees, a combination which forms the northern boundary. High cliffs face the rolling tides pushed up the Bristol Channel and from here Exmoor rises to a height of at least 700 feet (213 metres) with a large area above 1,000 feet (304 metres) and the dominant point being the open moorland around Dunkery Beacon which reaches 1,706 feet (520 metres).

The North Atlantic Drift, which is a branch of the Gulf Stream, ensures that warm sea breezes keep the climate warmer than one might imagine for an upland area with an annual rainfall in excess of 150 cms (60 inches), and which has more than its share of snow. Thus some quite exotic plants are able to survive along the coastal strip including the spring squill and even the high points of Exmoor can be botanically interesting. Peat, however, did develop on the impervious soils of the high moors and sphagnum moss occurs in the wetter areas along with typical acid upland plants such as sundew, bog asphodel and the cotton grasses.

During the 18th and 19th centuries trees were planted on the uplands these being mainly beech, larch, spruce ad pine although few have grown normally and many are stunted and twisted by wind action. There were some successes, however, and a beechwood planted by the Knights around Birch Cleave near Simonsbath in the 19th century at an altitude of over 1,000 feet (304 metres) is almost certainly the highest beech wood in Britain.

Botanists have divided Exmoor into three areas, each determined by its own dominant vegetation. To the north and around the coast the soil is shallow, well drained and quite acid.

Some of Britain's finest red deer stags occur on Exmoor.

The vegetation here is mainly heaths and gorse with both common and western gorse occurring. As their flowering periods overlap these areas seldom lack colour. There are problems with this habitat in the modern world as land has been claimed for farming and for building. There has also been deliberate burning of scrubland which has allowed excessive erosion.

The second area is made up of only about 8,400 hectares (21,000 acres) of heather moor which, as tourism increases, comes under even greater pressure. It is rather good agricultural soil which is also something of a premium on Exmoor. Included in this habitat is Dunkery Beacon where accidental fires can occasionally be a problem for the sensitive plants which include ling, bell heather and cross-leaved heath.

The central and third area of the moor is by far the largest and coincides more or less with the boundaries of the original Royal Forest. It is dominated by purple moorgrass which in the early autumn looks at its most attractive. This species covers around 4,000 hectares (10,000 acres) which is around a third of Exmoor but erosion is still a worry especially around the car parks. There are also substantial areas of mat grass and bracken. Although pretty to look at in the autumn and in winter this does tend to be ignored by sheep and can thus grow high enough to prevent light reaching the ground flora.

There is not much blanket-bog on Exmoor but there are a good number of areas dominated by cotton grass and efforts are being made to conserve what remains. It is certainly not being too pessimistic to say that many plants native to Exmoor are in some danger of extinction; between 1930 and 1970 more than 50 plants disappeared from the National Park and its surroundings.

In this respect the work of the Exmoor Natural History Society is to be commended and for many years bands of amateur but still highly-skilled botanists have sallied forth onto the moor armed with detailed maps and up-to-date equipment and methods. More than 800 species of plant have been mapped, but more work remains to be done.

Plants will only grow where they find the soil suitable and this in turn depends upon the underlying rocks. Many learned books have been written about the geology of the area, but for those who just wish to enjoy discovering Exmoor a brief idea of its make-up will suffice.

Unlike the high masses of land around Dartmoor, Exmoor lacks the great intrusions of exposed granite but is composed of layers of hard sedimentary rocks deposited as ancient seas evaporated or retreated while the climate changed over millions of years; such rocks include sandstone, slate and limestone. The actual structure can be seen at several exposed points especially in the coastal strip between Minehead and Baggy Point.

There have also been many books written about the animal life on Exmoor with its sheltered areas of moorland providing the ideal habitat for reptiles such as common lizard, slow-worm and adder, Britains only poisonous snake. The heathery uplands also provide a breeding habitat for birds such as the wheatear and whinchat and rarities which include the Dartford warbler and the mainly nocturnal nightjar. Above the treeline among the brackeny slopes the summer-visiting ring ouzel breeds; this was once called the mountain blackbird and does indeed resemble the blackbird except the ring ouzel has a prominent white crescent around the upper breast. Where there are farms the barn owl can occasionally be seen, probably due to the fact that this is not an area producing arable crops and in the 1960s the land was not sprayed with pesticides as were the more fertile soils of Britain. In hindsight it is now possible to see the damage done by such ill-thought-out treatments. In the damper areas several rare dragonflies occur including the emperor and the golden banded. Butterflies include the silver studded blue and the

The Dartford Warbler – one of Devon's rarest breeding birds.

grayling. For those who want to watch these insects then a hot summer's day is ideal but for those who wish to photograph them it is best to rise early and be at the swampy places when the first warm rays of sunlight strike the vegetation. The insects, being cold blooded, need to warm up their muscles before they can move quickly and at these times they are likely to spread their wings to soak up the warmth and so are relatively easy to observe and photograph. Likewise after a cold shower of rain – not infrequent in these parts – there may need to be another period of warming of the flight muscles.

The valleys running down from the hills are tree lined and here also are butterflies, including the brimstone which comes out of hibernation very early and can be on the wing during March, the female keeping a look out for leaves of Jack-by-the-Hedge on which she lays her eggs. The wooded valleys in spring are a riot of colours as wood anemone, primrose, and bluebell overlap each other in their flowering period. The variety of deciduous trees including oak, ash, birch and hawthorn attract many breeding birds especially along the Barle Valley and at Horner Wood. We have kept a list over the years and have noted the great spotted woodpecker, nuthatch, treecreeper, redstart and in recent years an increasing number of pied flycatcher. This is partly, but perhaps wholly, because of the provision of nest boxes in many of the woodlands managed by the National Trust and the Forestry Commission. The two most common birds of prey in these habitats are the sparrowhawk and the buzzard. Mammals include the badger which is refreshingly common in and around Exmoor.

Running down through these valleys are the fast-flowing rivers and both the dipper and the grey wagtail are typical residents here. Devon, however, is one of England's large refuges for the declining otter and Henry Williamson's *Tarka the Otter* was written as a result of his lifelong fascination with the species encountered along the rivers of Devon, especially the Taw and the Torridge; he also knew the Exmoor Waters well. Chapter 14 of *Tarka the Otter* is based on Exmoor with the animal hero disturbed at Pinkworthy (pronounced 'pinkery') Pond by a stag hunt. Tarka then went over the Chains to Hoaroak Water and on to its junction with the East Lyn River. From Watersmeet he then crossed country to Beggar's Roost and Inkerton Water. The writing proves that Henry Williamson obviously knew the route well and Exmoor lovers could do much worse than follow in his and Tarka's footsteps. Occasionally the swift Exmoor waters pause for breath and in the deep pools lurk fish easily seen by the kingfisher who chooses an overhanging branch from which to dive in pursuit of prey.

The coastline of North Devon should never be underrated by naturalists and for those with the time to spare the coastal path, or at least parts of this long-distance footpath, should be strolled along and savoured rather than walked just for the sake of exercise. Look out for the blue of spring squill, the vast drifts of purple thrift, the yellow of golden samphire and the delicate blue of harebell. Sit and wait patiently in the morning sun for butterflies like the pearl fritillary and small tortoiseshells which are common, whilst in some years continental migrants include the common red admiral and the much rarer clouded yellow and

The delightful little treecreeper occurs in the woodlands in and around Exmoor.

painted lady. The cliff tops around Heddon's Mouth and Woody Bay attract an assortment of breeding seabirds including guillemot, razorbill, herring and lesser black-backed gull and an increasing number of fulmar. Sadly the number of puffins breeding around the coast of Exmoor has declined drastically whilst the once common chough, a member of the crow family with a long, curved and delicate red bill has apparently gone for ever. On the positive side the breeding population of the peregrine is steadily increasing.

Wherever the natural history of Exmoor is discussed, however, two species above all others must take precedence – the Exmoor pony and the red deer. Most scientists believe the Exmoor pony to be a direct descendant of a wild horse which survived the ice-age. Actually the area which is now Somerset, Devon and Cornwall was fractionally below the ice although, of course, it would have been pretty cold and unpleasant in such a place. No one who has watched these tough horses facing winter weather can doubt that their resilience or independent spirit would make them excellent survivors. They are quite able to chew the tough moorland vegetation and scientists point out that they have a curved and specially thickened jawbone which has obviously evolved in response to this diet.

Although some interbreeding with 'domesticated' horses has occurred there are plenty of pure bred Exmoors about which can be recognised by a bay, dun or brown colour each with an oatmeal colouration in the area of the eyes and muzzle. During the winter Exmoors grow an extra thick coat of insulating fur and so efficient is this that observers have seen snow on their back completely unmelted and therefore acting like a natural blanket and retaining the body heat beneath. There is also a layer of long greasy hairs on the surface which is an ideal water repellent. We once watched a small herd of Exmoors near Tarr Steps sheltering beneath hawthorns during a January storm with sleet driving across the moor. The animals looked perfectly at east despite the fact that icicles were hanging from their muzzles. Their strength, endurance and the fact that they are of the few small breeds which can carry a man with ease has ensured their popularity with farmers over the centuries. Obviously interbreeding will dilute the natural strain but in 1980 the Exmoor National Park Authority set up two pure-bred herds which range around Hadden Hill, Warren Farm and East Anstey Common. The future of the Exmoor pony thus seems assured.

Human intervention over the last century has also ensured the survival of the red deer on Exmoor, and however much anti-hunting lobby may dislike it, this has been achieved only because of stag hunters.

Within the confines of the National Park is the largest herd of red deer outside Scotland. Britain's largest land mammal, the red deer is a formidable animal. Contrary to common belief the largest examples are found not in Scotland but on Exmoor where despite the tough habitat life is still not so exacting as in the Highlands of Scotland. The real Monarch of the Glen should perhaps be Monarch of the Combes! We were brought up in Cumbria and have watched the deer there and are familiar with the local language used to describe them – in Exmoor we found a different dialect applied to the red deer, especially the stags.

The life cycle of the Exmoor red begins with the birth of calves which is usually around the middle of June. The hind almost always produces a single calf and for the birth she selects a secluded spot, although the youngster is still agile within a surprisingly short period of time. The calves also have a spotted coat which provides a dappling effect which is excellent camouflage. Predators, particularly the fox, do not have colour vision and the contrast in light and shade of the spotted deer makes it almost impossible for them to be seen. Some also say that young deer do not emit much scent in their early days, and the dappling camouflage may continue until October in some cases. The calf is totally dependent upon the hind until the late autumn and even after being weaned the maternal bond may last well into the following year although the calf can survive should anything happen to the hind. Young females gradually become integrated into the social system but the development of a stag is much more dramatic and because of the growth of the antlers is much more obvious. In the past there has been some confusion, even among some otherwise competent naturalists, between antlers and horns. Antlers are bone-like structures originating from cylindrical bumps on the skull called pedicles. The antlers are solid and grow afresh each year, draining food supplies which at times must be somewhat limited. Horns on the other hand are permanent and composed of a firm outer skin growing around a soft inner cone richly supplied with nerves and blood vessels.

In some parts of their range red stags have been observed to eat shed antlers, but this does not appear to have been observed among those on Exmoor. Despite this annual loss the antlers increase in complexity from year to year and this has led to another erroneous assumption that they can be used as an accurate assessment of the age of an individual animal. It is said that antlers gain one point each year and all that one has to do to assess age is count the points. In fact the size of the antlers and the number of points depends upon several factors; age is certainly one, but the quantity and quality of available food, especially its calcium and phosphorus content are also important. Inheritance is another vital factor. It is therefore possible for those with years of experience of a particular herd in an area to look at a head of antlers and make an accurate assessment of the stag's age, although the observer may well know each individual anyway.

On Exmoor the stags lose their antlers between the end of April and the end of May with the older animals tending to shed their antlers earlier, perhaps because they are heavier. When an antler has been shed its replacement is almost immediately apparent as a rather painful-looking lump on the pedicle which grows very quickly, the delicate new tissues being protected by a substance known as velvet. There is still sensitivity at this point and the stag avoids contact with hard surfaces. As the antlers become mature, usually towards the end of August, the blood supply within the velvet dries up and when the velvet begins to fray it becomes an irritant. This is when stags can cause damage to trees by rubbing their antlers against sensitive bark and this 'fraying' is a source of annoyance to foresters. Occasionally there is a male stag which does not develop antlers and these are known as 'hummels' in Scotland, but in Exmoor they are called 'Notts'.

The rut, or breeding season, begins around the middle of October and lasts for about five weeks, but roaring or 'belling' stags have been observed in mid-September and as late as the end of January. As September progresses and their antlers look at their most impressive the herds of stags become increasingly restless and then aggressive, which results in males becoming solitary and beginning to roar in order to establish territory. We have known stags at this time become very aggressive towards human beings but in our experience these have been parkland animals which look upon humans as rivals. In the wild observers are not likely to be attacked. The males, however, are very aggressive to each other and fights are often bloody and occasionally lead to death. A male stag at the peak of fitness is a formidable beast both to look at and listen to and even to smell! Apart from the antlers the neck becomes heavily muscled, the roaring echoes over the hills for a considerable distance, and frequent rolling in mud partly created by the stag's urine produces an unforgettable smell. We once came across such a rutting pool and the smell of ammonia was so strong that it made our eyes water. In Exmoor these areas are known as 'spoiling pits' and some local experts feel that apart from the scent given by the mud they may also be of value in keeping the stags cool. At this

Around the drier areas close to wet patches provides the ideal habitat for Britain's only poisonous snake – the adder.

time a dominant stag may stand as high as 4 feet (1.2 metres) at the shoulder and be able to attract, hold and fertilise a harem of as many as 15 hinds. During this time he feeds little, fights frequently, mates as often as he can and at the end of the rut he will be very tired and in need of a good rest. In view of the tough life that they lead it is surprising that deer often reach the age of 15 and specimens living more than 20 years are by no means unusual.

Whenever the red deer of Exmoor are discussed the thorny subject of stag-hunting arises which many find so abhorrent that they alter the truth in order to make political capital. We would never feel at ease hunting ourselves but cannot ignore the one very obvious fact that without hunting the red deer would soon become extinct. In 1825 after almost a century of hunting the deer were not easy to find and the one remaining pack of hounds was sold to a German. Without the hunt poachers began to shoot the remaining deer and by 1855 it was estimated that fewer than 50 animals were to be found over the whole of Exmoor. An unsuccessful attempt was made to re-establish the hunt at this time but things did not improve and in 1900 the Devon and Somerset Staghounds were established on a very firm basis. One of the packs now hunts a total of eight times each week. Objectors forget that a hunt either catches or misses its quarry, and their officials patrol Exmoor in an effort to prevent shooting which maims more animals than it kills cleanly and without suffering. In the days of high powered rifles with telescopic sights, however, culling by marksmen could be an answer. Those who know little about the habits of red deer and nothing whatever about Exmoor ask the naive question 'Why cull the deer at all?' The moor is not just an area of heather but a complex mixture of open land, woods and farmland and in may cases owner occupied as opposed to being part of the National Park. Both foresters and farmers suffer from the activities of deer but they also know that the animals are now a tourist attraction. The answer has therefore been found in compromise and the hunt keeps the numbers of deer in check and yet ensures the survival of the species. The farmers enjoy the sport, visitors fill the hotels and enjoy watching the preparations for that hunt if not the hunt itself. Neither must it be forgotten that many local jobs depend upon the continuance of the hunt including blacksmiths and those who care for the hounds.

Whatever one feels about the ethics of hunting it is a colourful part of Exmoor which has done more than many naturalists admit to preserve the wildlife of the area.

CHAPTER 2

Around Dulverton

Newcomers to Exmoor should begin with a visit to the National Park Centre at the Old Workhouse at Dulverton and talk to the friendly staff who are only too pleased to help.

The town itself serves as the shopping centre for the south-eastern corner of Exmoor and it has held this position since the 13th century although it is still a small town of jumbled buildings, a limited number of well-stocked and interesting shops and with excellent parking. It is squeezed between high hills and is close to the junction of Exmoor's two main rivers, the Exe and the Barle, which flows through the town itself. Both rivers offer good fishing and the Barle Valley is particularly noted for its woodlands which fascinate naturalists. Here we have watched the occasional otter and badger and much more regularly observed dipper and grey wagtail throughout the year and common sandpiper in the summer.

In *Lorna Doone,* Jan Ridd and his servant John Fry enjoyed a meal of mutton at an inn in Dulverton and there are several inns which can still provide an excellent bar meal including the Lion with gilded lions guarding the entrance, the Lamb with its animal looking out over the street from its Ionic portico, the Bridge and the Rock. Cream teas are sold at a number of genteel little cafés which do a roaring trade during the all too short tourist season.

Dulverton has several literary connections including a locally famous resident, Dr Charles Park Collyns (1793-1864). After being educated at Blundell's school at Tiverton he established himself as a surgeon-apothecary in 1814. He seems to have been very young for such a post but no doubt he improved. We wonder what his patients thought of the young man in the early years of his practice. A keen hunting man, Collyns could also write with great feeling and his *The Chase of the Wild Deer* published in the 1840s became a classic. Richard Jefferies visited Dulverton in 1883 and no doubt read Collyns's book whilst researching his own monograph *The Red Deer.* In this there is a lovely description of the river which is one of our favourite pieces of writing about the natural world.

'The brown Barle splashes in the sunshine like boys bathing - like them he is sunburnt and brown. He laughs and talks, and sings louder than the wind in his woods.'

W. H. Hudson followed the River Exe and he used similar words by pointing out that it 'sings all the way to Dulverton'. Other literary figures who visited the town in addition to Blackmore and those already mentioned include Tennyson, who stayed at Brushford, and William Wordsworth, who with his sister Dorothy tramped the area with their friend Coleridge.

Some writers have remarked that Dulverton lacks any buildings of distinction, but they do some injustice to the town hall and to All Saints Parish Church. Although the interior was somewhat spoiled by an insensitive 1852 restoration around the 13th century tower, the exterior is impressive especially when viewed from the town through the lych-gate. From this angle the church can be seen to have been built on the summit of a hill with the delightful jumble of buildings constructed at its feet. The huge sycamore called the belfry tree which once dominated the churchyard is now truncated, showing signs of its age and is dying back with each passing year. It may well be 200 years old. During 1991 the Guildhall, situated between the main street and the National Park Centre was restored from a near ruinous condition.

From Dulverton there are attractive walks to the few remaining ruins of Barlinch Priory some 1½ miles north-east of the town to the west of the road to Minehead. Also worth a visit is Pixton situated about a mile from Dulverton. Here lived Sir Thomas Acland, a keen hunting man who owned Exmoor's first pack of stag hounds during the 18th century.

Dulverton is also the best base from which to explore Tarr Steps which many feel to be the finest multiple clapper bridge in England, being 180 feet (55 metres) long and with 17 spans. The steps are reached by turning along a cul-de-sac signed from the road between Dulverton and Withypool. There is a spacious car park with neat clean toilets, a signed footpath leading down to the River Barle and each stile has been adapted to allow easy passage for dogs. In the summer a farm overlooking the steps serves particularly good snacks. Close to the steps is what is described as a 'deep ford'. We have visited the steps in the driest

Hunting is a harder business than often realised. Individuals get separated from the huntsman whose lonely job is to isolate the quarry. At the end of the day man and beast are physically exhausted and the deer invariably escapes.

of weathers and even then we would be very reluctant to cross in a saloon car. For those wanting refreshment at the Tarr Steps' Hotel it is best to cross the bridge on foot or journey back to the main road and approach the river from the opposite side. Scholars have disagreed about the origins of the bridge which is made up of huge blocks of gritstone which some say dates to the Bronze Age, due to the presence of nearby burial sites. Most folk, however, think that Tarr Steps are medieval in origin. All discount the legend that this is the devil's bridge, which he built in order to indulge in a spot of sunbathing despite the fact that this region is much cooler than his normal habitat! A parson sent to confront him was sworn at, but the cleric matched the devil curse for curse. This so impressed the devil that he gave free passage over the Barle whilst retaining his rights to sunbathe.

During severe storms the bridge does not escape damage and the middle sections were washed away during 1941-42 and the whole structure was almost demolished in 1952 and again in 1979. On a tranquil day of high summer we love to dangle our feet in the cool waters of the Barle before following part of the footpath towards Winsford which is some five miles away. The dominant riverside trees are alder and willow with an understorey of many plants including hard fern, butterbur, ground ivy and foxglove. Pheasants seem to be everywhere but the birdlife of the whole area is always of interest including redstart, long-tailed tit, and wood warbler, with sparrowhawks and buzzard being common and the hobby an occasional summer visitor.

For motorists as opposed to walkers there is a delightful route to Wimbleball, a distance of around six miles. The route crosses the Exe river at Hele Bridge and onto the junction of the A396 which connects Minehead to Exeter. A right turn along this road is followed for around ¾ mile before a left turn indicates Bury and Watchet.

Although not much more than a hamlet, Bury, now snuggled into the valley of the little River Haddeo, was once as important as its name implies. Bury means a fortified place and the outline of the old motte and bailey can still be seen at the top of the hill surrounded by a bluebell wood and from which are splendid views down the junction of the Haddeo with the Exe.

There are walks from Bury alongside the River Haddeo which is spanned by a packhorse bridge and then onward and upward to Wimbleball Lake. Beyond the lake the river's course can be followed again onto the slopes of Haddon Hill which is 353 metres (1160 feet) above sea level. The lake was formed by damming the waters of the Haddon. Close to the dam it can be seen that the waters of another little river called the Pulham also feed the lake. Those visiting Wimbleball by car should turn right at Bury along a narrow winding lane signposted Skilgate and Watchet. This leads to a junction at Frogwell Cross. Turn left along the B3190 signed Upton and Watchet and continue the sign for Wimbleball Lake, where there is a substantial car park and picnic site. To reach the lake a path leads downhill for about ½ mile to a flight of steps leading to the viewing platform. Disabled drivers are able to drive down to a small car park much closer to the lake and from where there are splendid views. Wimbleball is the perfect example of multiple use of water with fishing, yachting, canoeing, wind surfing, rowing and birdwatching all encouraged. The lake is 200 metres (656 feet) above sea level and occupies 374 acres surrounded by some 500 acres of woodland and meadows. The Somerset Trust for Nature Conservation manage 29 acres at the northern tip of the lake as a Nature reserve and leaflets describing the area can be bought at the café-shop near Bessom Bridge. This is open daily from Easter to the end of October and then at weekends until Christmas.

Tarr Steps is one of the finest clapper bridges in Britain, but historians are divided with regard to its origins.

From 1st May to the end of October a site for 30 tents and three motor campers is open although there is no accommodation for caravans.

The disabled are particularly well catered for at Wimbleball and a boat has been adapted to take wheelchairs and can be booked in advance from the warden as can a well-appointed lecture room which seats about 30 people. The latter is very popular with groups of naturalists.

Before returning to Dulverton, two attractive villages which must be visited are Upton and Brompton Regis. Upton is a straggle of a village on the side of Haddon Hill which was well known to the old cattle drovers who rested at the Lowtrow Cross Inn whilst their animals cropped grass in the local fields. There is a rather plain 19th-century church, but the real fame of the village is based upon a battered tower which now stands forlorn and close to Upton farm. This is all that remains of the church which was almost demolished in 1867 and thankfully the tower resisted a demolition order in 1971. An unconfirmed story suggests that the tower was used as a refuge by Charles Lindbergh and his wife and son following the kidnapping of their 20-month-old child. Whether this is true or not it makes a grand tale. A walk from the village leads to the source of the Haddeo to the north-east of Vennie House.

Nearby Brompton Regis is at its best in late summer when the purple heather is a delight both to see and to smell. Brompton Regis was once the largest settlement in the area and had every right to be called a market town. St. Mary's Church has a sturdy west tower constructed in the 13th century, with the north aisle in the Perpendicular style constructed around 1520. It did, however, suffer greatly from Victorian vandals who described themselves as architects. The central furnishings of St. Mary's were ripped out including a singers' gallery, box pews and a fan-vaulted rood screen. The latter was not chopped up but eventually sold to a dealer in Tiverton around 1860. What a shame that such joys are lost for ever to this grand old church.

Opposite the church are two old cottages, plus the site of the old village pump which is now replaced by a large tap. Another reminder of past glories is the white-painted George Inn which serves a variety of bar snacks and good ales which are much better than the water from the pump. Near this is a plaque dated 1870 and inscribed with the words 'Whosoever drinketh of this water shall thirst again, but he that drinketh of Me shall never thirst.'

The history of the settlement goes back to Saxon times when it was called Bruneton meaning 'a settlement within the Brendon Hills'. It was owned by King Harold's mother Girtha. It was only natural that her lands should be taken by William the Conqueror following Harold's death at Hastings in 1066. It became the King's settlement of Bruneton Regis which evolved eventually into Brompton Regis and was given to William de Saye who founded Barlynch Priory. Perhaps if Harold had been victorious, Bruneton would have become a vital cog in local history instead of Dulverton or Tiverton. This we shall never know.

CHAPTER 3

Tiverton to South Molton – The Gateway to Exmoor

Parking in Tiverton can, at times, be a nightmare but the town itself is a place of sweet dreams. Visitors approaching the town from Taunton may find some parking space close to St. Peter's Parish Church which will save entering the one-way system which to the uninitiated can be a problem.

We parked by the church on a Saturday morning of January sunshine to hear the sound of churchbells greeting the arrival of a bride; silence for a while followed by the sound of Mendlessohn's 'Wedding March'. Few people realise that this was not written as wedding music, but was entitled 'A Midsummer Night's Dream'. It was first adapted as nuptial music by Samuel Wreay the organist of St. Peter's and it was therefore a Tiverton bride who was first greeted by the 'Wedding March'.

The church itself has its own glories on offer, and to the right of the imposing entrance are a set of delightful carvings restored in 1983 and showing Elizabethan ships. Inland Tiverton may be – its name derives from the Saxon Twyford-tun, – the two ford town – but one of its greatest sons made his fortune from the sea. John Greenway was born around 1460 and when he died in 1529 he was rich and Tiverton was famous. From a little village with its local family, the Courtenays, devastated by the Wars of the Roses, Tiverton rode on the crest of an industrial wave dominated by wool. Perhaps the time was right for the rising merchant classes to take over from the noble families who had in many cases been killed in battles or executed for failing either the Lancastrian or Yorkist kings as power see-sawed from one to the other.

John Greenway, once a poor boy in Tiverton, did not forget his native town and paid for a chantry chapel to be built in the church and also for the alms houses which still stand, although they were restored in 1732. They are difficult to photograph or study in detail because of traffic. The carvings on the outside of the church tell John Greenway's life story. His fortune was made from the manufacture of kersey which became increasingly popular in the last half of the 15th century, and was actually made

North Molton Church.

in local cottages, with merchants like Greenway buying all they could produce. English broadcloth was a very heavily felted material usually dyed in a very dark colour. Kersey was produced in the west of England using a coarser and lighter wool which could be dyed in rich reds, blues and greens which appealed to the increasingly fashion-conscious people beginning to relax in the peace of Tudor England after centuries of war. The West Country clothiers also managed to break free of the restrictive practices drawn up by the merchant guilds. In 1486 the Merchant Adventurers were instituted and this meant that the Fellowship of Drapers, including John Greenway, could protect themselves against piracy by building their own armed vessels. This explains the Tudor galleons accurately carved on the exterior of the church.

St. Peter's, of cathedral-like proportions, was founded in 1073, but the main body today is 15th century with the soaring west tower being typical of West Country churches and known as 'Somerset Style'. Many church aficianados have described the interior as disappointing but the Norman doorway is certainly impressive as are the tombs of the wool merchants, John Waldron and George Slee, which are worth travelling a long way to see. Just as Greenway gave alms houses so did George Slee, and John Waldron. Slees' Jacobean-style mansion known as the Great House, which still stands in St. Peter's Street, was built in 1613 and is now used as the council offices whilst the alms houses he built are close by. Slees' table-top tomb is a fine monument to yet another self-made Tiverton wool merchant. Waldron's alms-houses were built in 1579 for eight poor persons and their wooden gallery is typical of the period. These are situated near Heathcoat's Social Club.

Tiverton Castle, which stands on the same wooded knoll as the church above the River Exe, dates from 1106 when King Henry I made Richard de Redvers the Earl of Devon with orders to construct a castle and it has been inhabited ever since. It is open to the public from Easter to the end of September, Monday to Thursday from 2.30 to 5.30 pm. Visitors enter through the medieval main gate which was once defended by a drawbridge and portcullis, with details of the long-drained moat still apparent. Then comes a peaceful courtyard and garden which always seems silent despite the close proximity of the modern road into the town. There is a fine collection of Civil War arms, and a bewildering assortment of clocks ticking away like mad and an exhibition of Victorian murder mysteries.

In the late 16th century the castle was in the hands of the Royalist-supporting Gifford family and during the Civil War they held firm for Charles I, but in 1645 Sir Thomas Fairfax the Parliamentarian general captured the castle and demolished its fortifications. An earlier reminder of the history of Tiverton is the Joan of Arc gallery commemorating a relative of the Campbell family who then owned the castle, and who was the martyr's chief military advisor.

Another magnificent castle is situated four miles from Tiverton on the Exeter road. Bickleigh Castle is open during Easter and then on Wednesdays, Sundays and Bank Holidays up to the Spring Bank Holiday. Between then and October it opens daily except Saturdays from 2 pm to 5 pm. The entry fee includes a tour of the castle buildings, some of which have been lived in since the 12th century, a maritime exhibition and what is referred to as a spy escape display relating to the Second World War, particularly enjoyed by children. Here also are Tudor furniture and paintings plus the story of Sir George Carew, a vice-admiral who lived here and was once in charge of the famous ship, *Mary Rose.* More modern displays include agricultural implements, armour and toys. There is a shop and a good refreshment area plus the 'spooky tower' which children can climb and old rocking horses which they can ride. Our favourite place is the 11th-century thatched chapel which is said to be the oldest complete building in Devon.

More details of the history of Tiverton and district can be discovered by descending into the town centre to the Tiverton Museum housed in the restored 19th-century national school on St Andrew Street. Entry to the museum is free although donations are requested. The opening times are as follows: from February to December, Monday to Saturday 10.30 am to 4.30 pm, and also on bank holidays. The museum is closed on Sundays even during the holiday season and from 24th December to 31 January although it will open for pre-arranged visits. In our travels around the country we have visited many such museums set up by so-called amateurs and their enthusiasm always shines through. No wonder the Tiverton Museum has received many national accolades for its collections, which include a complete village smithy and wheelwright's shop, local history, costume, furniture, documents, agricultural implements, clocks, naval and aircraft models, wildlife displays and a huge number of local photographs. The shop reflects all these displays. Any story of Tiverton must include railway exhibits and details of the textile industry. The railway gallery houses the steam locomotive which once ran on the Exe Valley line until its closure and which is painted in the green livery of the Great Western Railway.

Tiverton should not be mentioned without reference to lace making which actually saved the town when the woollen trade fell on hard times. The bobbinet lace-making machine was designed and built by John Heathcote, who established his company in Tiverton in 1816. He came from Leicestershire because the Luddites were trying to destroy his invention which was much less labour intensive than other machines in use and many hand lace makers feared for their jobs. Heathcote established his lace factory in a disused woollen mill on the banks of the River Exe and the enterprise is still the largest employer in the area although now part of the Coats Paton Group. Tiverton lace is invariably used to embellish royal wedding gowns. There is a factory shop which is open from 9.30 am to 4.30 pm from Monday to Friday and from 9 am to 6 pm on Saturday. It proves very popular in the holiday season when visitors are on the look out for a special present to take back to a loved one.

A short but fairly steep walk leads from the town centre to the Grand Western Canal basin on Canal Hill, passing Lowman Bridge near which is an ornate clock tower and statue of Edward VII which were given to the town by Thomas Ford in the early years of the 20th century. Just beyond Lowman's is Old Blundell's, a grammar school founded in 1604 by Peter Blundell, yet another Tiverton merchant who made his fortune from the manufacture of kerseys. He died in 1601 and left money in his will to build a school 'as near the river of Exe or Lowman as maybe'. The Lowman is a tributary of the Exe. Today the school is situated about a mile away along Blundell's Road, with the old school maintained by the National Trust. Although the building itself is not open to the public it is possible to enter through a fine set of gates and look at the Elizabethan exterior, in front of which is a triangular lawn. It was this which R. D. Blackmore described in the introductory chapter of *Lorna Doone.* He called the triangle 'the ironing box' and it was here that John Ridd was fighting Robin Snell when John Fry, the family servant, arrived to take John home where he would be told that the Doones had killed his father. Apart from Blackmore Blundell's had other famous sons including 'Jack' Russell the hunting parson who bred the terrier which now bears his name and also Archbishop Temple, one of the most loved of those who held the see of Canterbury. A famous headmaster was Samuel Wesley, brother of John, and he guided the school briefly around 1739.

The Grand Western Canal Basin is now the focus for a developing country park and a company called 'Welcome Aboard' run horse-drawn and motor boat cruises between May and September. At the peak of the season pre-booking is usually essential but it is worth the effort as not many canal trips last as long as 1$^1/_2$ hours and actually pass through a lock. The idea of the Grand Western Canal was to link the Bristol Channel, or the Severn Sea as it was then called, with the English Channel. The 30-mile cut was planned from near Taunton in Somerset to Topsham just south of Exeter and on a navigable portion of the River Exe. It was also in the minds of the planners to cut a branch

The parish church at Molland, once an important halt on the turnpike road to Exeter.

from Burlescombe to Tiverton, but finance was always a problem. Only the section from Taunton to Burlescombe and then the Tiverton branch were built, the latter section being opened in 1814, although the increasing financial problems meant that the final link was only made to Taunton in 1838. Even then the last section was done very much on the cheap and was constructed to a smaller gauge which was only suitable for tub-boats and totally useless for barges. The main income came from carrying stone and limestone by horse-drawn tubs from the Burlescombe quarries to Tiverton. By the time the Grand Western came into modest profit in the 1840s the Bristol to Exeter railway was built, took away trade and in 1853 the canal was leased to the railway company. In 1924 no business was done at all although in the 1960s it was still owned by British Rail and serious consideration was given to filling in the canal. In 1962 the Tiverton Preservation Society was formed, its hard work saved the Great Western and in 1971 the Devon County Council joined in. A half mile section near Halberton was flooded and there is now 11¼ miles of water between Tiverton and Holcombe Rogus on the Somerset/Devon border. This is one of the most attractive country parks in Britain.

From Tiverton the A396 road heads towards Bampton and then into the heart of Exmoor but just two miles north of Tiverton is Knightshayes Court. This is open between 1st April and 31st October with the garden open from 11 am to 6 pm and the house from 1.30 pm to 6 pm. It is closed on Fridays. Knightshayes was built by William Burges in 1870 for John Heathcote Amory the M.P. for Tiverton and grandson of the lacemaking founder. Here is one of the finest gardens in Devon with imaginative topiary, rare trees and shrubs, plus colourful flowers providing a show at all times of the year. The contents of the house includes paintings, china and furniture given by Lady Amory but supplemented by the National Trust who now administer the house although the family remains in residence. The Trust have run the house since the death of the second Sir John Amory in 1972. There is a gift shop, licensed restaurant with coffees, lunches and teas available. Plants can also be purchased. There is a picnic area close to the car park and disabled visitors are particularly well catered for.

Bampton is another colourful spot which won a 'Britain in Bloom' award in 1989. Many settlements describe themselves as

One of the observation hives at the honey farm in South Molton.

the gateway to somewhere, but Bampton actually does lie on the borders of Exmoor. The narrow valleys typical of the high moor begin to broaden here on the banks of the pretty little river Batherm, a tributary of the Exe. Once each year the peace is disrupted but nobody minds as the October Exmoor pony sale takes over the town.

The plain stone Georgian cottages are not typical of Devonshire thatch but add a rugged friendliness to the place which is overlooked by the large church of St. Michael. There was a church at Bampton by AD 712 and it belonged to the monks of Glastonbury Abbey. There is documentary evidence supporting the fact that Abbot Bernwald was burned below the altar of St Michael's. It is possible that there was a pagan settlement here because it was customary to name pagan sites after St Michael as he was the archangel who cast down Satan. Two ancient, perhaps even Bronze Age, tracks cross at Bampton. One runs from the Channel coast near Exeter to Minehead on the Bristol Channel; the other from the Midlands over the Blackdown Hills through Wellington, on to South Molton and then onwards to Barnstaple. The Batherm was forded here and for those with time to spare the old tracks can still be followed as footpaths through picturesque countryside.

The history of Bampton's church moved swiftly on following William's Conquest and he gave the Saxon manor to one of his favourite knights, Walter of Douai. The monks of Glastonbury offended the new owner in some way and Walter gave the living to Bath Abbey and in the 15th century yet another monastery was given to Bampton, this time Buckland Abbey near Tavistock.

The interior of St Michael and All Angels has many points of interest including the fine 14th-century porch, a Norman window which is even earlier and roofs which are typically West Country in design being of the waggon type of carved oak which is withstanding the passage of time with graceful yet solid strength. In the chancel which mainly dates from the 14th century is a fine piscina in which the communal vessels were washed. The medieval window close to the south door shows the coats of arms of local families of the time including the Shapcotes, the Fitzwarrens and the Dinhams. It is a fine example of the glassmakers' art dated about 1495. There is also a Jacobean pulpit and on it are carvings including Jack in Green, a throw back to the pagan times when worshipping things natural was the accepted practice.

Those wishing to tour the borders of Exmoor by car pass through the pretty little hamlet of Exbridge before reaching Brushford, on the River Barle, which gave the poet Tennyson such pleasure in 1891. He was over 80 at the time and was brought by his son by train, the pair staying at the Carnarvon Arms built in 1873 as a railway hotel. The rail link had long been closed but the hotel remains and much of the route can still be traced through Devon.

The hotel, however, still thrives and is used as a centre by anglers and walkers eager to explore the Haddon valley.

Enhancing the natural scenery is Combe Manor, a Tudor building built on an even older foundation, and it is alleged that Sir Francis Drake played bowls on the lawns at the rear of the house. This may well have been the case because the house belonged to the Sydenham family from 1540 to 1874 and Sir Francis's wife was Elizabeth Sydenham of Monksilver (see Chapter 10) who was a cousin of the Brushford Sydenhams.

Silver and lead were mined on the estate until the end of the 18th century and added to the family prosperity. Some members of the family, including Humphey who was vicar of Brushford in the 1630s and 1640s, were generous to the church which is dedicated to St Nicholas. The churchyard is dominated by a venerable old oak tree which is so weakened by age that it is now firmly propped up to maintain its contact with the church. Inside there is a 12th-century font, some French and Flemish stained glass, a fine 15th-century rood screen and a chapel designed by Lutyens. This is a memorial to Colonel Aubrey Herbert, a soldier and a scholar, whose life was used by John Buchan as a basis for his character Sandy Arbuthnot, the hero of his novel *Greenmantle.*

The road from Brushford to South Molton pushes through some of the finest scenery on the fringes of Exmoor passing Old Ways End, East Anstey and the Five Crossways boundary continuing over Anstey Common. This is horse-riding country, the bridle paths twisting and turning around the wetter areas of the dark peaty soil. Sweet smelling heathers in summer and driving snow in winter make this unpredictable country but this is why it is so attractive.

A look at a map reveals that the forest is roughly heart-shaped and is bordered by a number of parishes still separated by narrow, twisting roads. Before exploring South Molton four of these little parishes can be visited namely Twitchen, North Molton, Molland and Challacombe which form the western boundary. These are wild and windy places where farmers battle to make a living and naturalists watch the wildlife which also has to endure the Exmoor climate.

St Peter's Church at Twitchen was rebuilt in 1844 and apart from the tower is small and, unattractive to look at. But what character it has bracing itself against the elements like a terrier waiting outside a fox hole. Challacombe is another cold spot and there is an unsupported local story that the last two of the Doone family, an elderly member and his young granddaughter, were found dead hereabouts in the snow on the road to Simonsbath. They had apparently fallen on hard times and were singing carols around Challacombe for 'pennies'.

Holy Trinity Church is around a mile from the village and stands on the 900-foot summit of a windswept hill at Barton Town. Reaching this place by car is not easy as the road is narrow, overlooked by very high beech hedges and undulates to such an extent that sudden descents can lead to valleys which flood and the next minute a steep hill climb means the engagement of the lowest gear. Getting to church in these parts on a winter's day of blizzard in those days of horse transport must have been a problem at best and impossible from time to time. Failure to worship on the Sabbath was regarded as a mortal sin until very recent times.

North Molton is a huge parish of more than 15,000 acres stretching almost up to the borders of Exmoor. The Parish Church of All Saints dates from the late 14th century although there have been some alterations since. There is a medieval pulpit above which is a sounding board dating from the early years of the Hanoverian dynasty. There are two chapels of interest, the Bamfylkde sanctuary having a memorial to Sir Amyas who died in 1626 and his fertile wife Elizabeth who bore him 12 sons and five daughters. The family fortune was made from their copper mines at Heasley Mill just over a mile to the north-west of the village. The Parker Chapel is not so grand but has some fine medieval glass. Both South and North Molton are situated on the lovely River Mole, a tributary to the River Taw. This is a splendid otter river with attractive wooded dells and footpaths.

South Molton began as a Saxon village around AD 700 but became prosperous from the early Middle Ages as a centre for the wool trade, and the annual sheep fair which takes place in August dates back to 1357. The parish church dedicated to St Mary Magdalene was mentioned in the Domesday Book of 1086 and even then it was large enough to support four priests. The present building has a magnificent 15th-century tower standing at a height of 102 feet (31 metres) and visible for miles. Until 1751 there was a spire on top of the tower but at that time it was struck by lightning and not replaced. The interior is not very remarkable but there is an attractive pulpit of carved stone and some good examples of late Victorian stained glass windows. We always try to remember that age is sometimes thought to bestow beauty, and once these modern windows have the benefit of great age their qualities may well be viewed in a different light.

The town is sandwiched between the rugged hills of Exmoor and the pasturelands of mid-Devon, and was thus an ideal choice as a market centre. Broad Street is as wide as its name implies and here are to be found the signs of civic pride. The town hall built in 1740 overhangs the pavement with a balcony supported on four Greek-like pillars. The museum on the ground floor has an excellent collection of pewter, provides a comprehensive history of mining on Exmoor and on display are two fire engines, one of which is dated 1739. Behind curtains which can be drawn back are two beautifully written charters, one dated May 9th 1590 during the reign of Elizabeth I and the other given by Charles II and dated Christmas Eve 1684. Entry to the museum is free but donations are always welcome. It is closed on Sunday and Monday and during winter, with the opening period stretching from mid-March to late November. Also here is a massive cider press and it is fitting that Devon cider has been made locally for centuries. The Hancock family have been making the amber nectar for five generations and their Clapworthy Mill headquarters is situated only three miles from the town on the B3226 road to Exeter. The shop is open all the year round but tours are organised daily from Easter to the end of October except Sundays. An audiovisual film shows the autumn cider pressing off local apples, especially a variety called bitter sweet and there is a museum, craft shop, picnic area and of course a well-stocked off-license.

For those who prefer food rather than drink then South Molton has another treat to offer – the Quince Honey Farm. This is the largest exhibition of working honey bees in the world. It is open throughout the year, seven days a week, although the café only operates during the summer season. There are videos about the life history of the bees and how honey is marketed commercially. Safely working behind glass it is possible to approach the bees and photograph them even with the simplest of cameras. Visitors in search of unusual presents should spend some time in the shop which obviously sells honey, but also a great variety of products made from beeswax. In summer the three-acre picnic area can be busy but even in winter the honey

Tiverton Church was the first to use the Wedding March to greet a bride.

farm is one of North Devon's most fascinating places.

South Molton is also an ideal centre from which to visit four very contrasting places, namely the Cobbaton Combat Collection at Chittlehampton, the National Trust-owned house at Arlington Court, the Exmoor Steam Centre and the Exmoor Bird Gardens both at Bratton Fleming. For those interested in Parson Jack Russell and his territory a visit to Swimbridge to see his grave is of interest especially as the church has a splendid rood screen and pulpit.

When Preston Isaac founded his Cobbaton Museum he blamed it on a hobby which got out of hand. It is open from April 1st to the end of October seven days a week from 10 am to 6 pm. It can be visited in the off-peak season by appointment and is situated between Chittlehampton, which is six miles west of SouthMolton, and Umberleigh.

Although the museum has interesting tanks and weapons dating from the Second World War it is much more varied than a war museum – it is a stroll down memory lane. Older visitors come out whistling or humming 'Roll out the Barrel', 'Underneath the Arches' or 'The White Cliffs of Dover' whilst youngsters are taken back to the 1939-45 period when men fought hard, women worked just as hard in munition factories,

Old Blundells School, attended by R.D. Blackmore, is now owned by the National Trust and used as offices.

and all waited for bombs to fall but in the long evenings of waiting for the blitz people sang, danced and were happy. All who want such a glimpse into the past should come to Cobbaton.

Even if there was no museum it would be worth visiting Chittlehampton, just to see the parish church. This is dedicated to a Saxon lady named Urith who became St Hieritha and was born at Stowford, a mile to the north of the church. She was cut to pieces by the local heathens and it is said that:-

> 'Where the Holy Maiden fell
> Water gushed forth from a well
> And the dry earth blossomed.'

St Urith's Well is still there to the east of the village and it is said that a church was built around her grave. The present church dates from the late 15th century and the pulpit is of about the same age. It is carved in stone and depicts the lady herself holding a palm leaf symbolising martyrdom and also the foundation stone of the church. The 114-foot (35 metre) tower is magnificent and the local masons were quick to boast of its glory and local legend has it that of Devon churches 'Bishop's Nympton for length, South Molton for strength, but Chittlehampton for beauty'.

There is also plenty to see at the National Trust-owned Arlington Court which is more than just a house although it would still be worth it if this were the case. It is open daily except Saturdays (unless it happens to be a bank holiday) from Easter to September from 11 am to 6 pm but during October it closes at 5 pm. Arlington is situated close to the A39 and near to Blackmoor Gate.

The house was left to the National Trust by Miss Rosalie Chichester on her death in 1949. She had already organised the 3,471-acre (1388-hectare) estate into a nature reserve and this the Trust has retained. Close to the lake, on which an assortment of wildfowl occur, is a heronry and as these graceful birds nest early their breeding season is almost complete by the time Arlington opens for the season. The nature trails are worth a day to themselves as are the outdoor exhibits, including Shetland ponies and Jacob's sheep, whilst in the stables is a glittering display of 19th-century vehicles including a town coach for the gentry, another coach used for continental travel as well as 'local transport' such as broughams, gigs, victorias and pony-drawn bath chairs. The dawning of the age of the horseless carriage is not forgotten either with lots of early models on display.

The house was built to a design by Thomas Lee between 1820 and 1823 and it is not a particularly impressive structure from the outside but within it are treasures accumulated by the Chichesters who inhabited the Arlington site from the 14th century. This is not so much a stately home as a museum with collections of snuffboxes and silver, pewter, porcelain and paintings, books and bottled ships, fans and furniture plus one intangible and invaluable factor – atmosphere.

For those who enjoy their natural history at close quarters then a visit to the Exmoor Bird Garden is a must. It is situated on the B3226 midway between Blackmoor Gate and Bratton Fleming. It is open every day except Christmas Day from 10 am, closing at 6 pm between April and October and at 4 pm in winter. Most of the paths are so laid that they are easily suited to the disabled. Spread over 12 acres is Tarzan-land for the young and adventurous but there is serious natural history as well with over 500 species of birds and animals on display including a large collection of tropical birds which means there is a good display even in the grimmest of weather. There are also birds which thrive in cold weather including penguins and a good assortment of wildfowl. Many British species are kept here and thus those visitors beginning their studies will be able to learn the skills of identification. There is a picnic site in the grounds but for those who wish to sit in comfort there is a well-appointed café.

During the 1990s Bratton Fleming is likely to become an important venue for walking and railway enthusiasts as the Exmoor Steam Centre develops alongside the B3226. Exmoor Town Station gives some idea of what conditions were like when the narrow-gauge passenger railway ran from Barnstaple at Lynton as described in Chapter 7. From the White Hart Inn there is a series of circular walks which provide spectacular views, our favourite being towards Hartland Point. These routes should be described as strolls rather than walks and allow those touring by car to relax, have a picnic and return to their vehicles in around one hour.

CHAPTER 4

The Hidden Triangle of Mid to North Devon
Crediton to Bideford

One of our main problems in writing this book was to define where the influence of Exmoor ends and that of Dartmoor begins. After long discussions with helpful tourist information officers in Barnstaple and elsewhere we decided that Devonians accept that the border of the present book should be delineated by roads running from Crediton to Bideford and should also include the coastline around Clovelly. This is an area surprisingly little explored and which shows Devonshire farmland at its very best.

The best place to begin this journey is therefore at the Devonshire Centre at Bickleigh Mill situated on the A396 from Tiverton towards Exeter and close to the A3072 to Crediton. Bickleigh Bridge itself is a delightful structure, now a protected monument, and celebrated in Simon and Garfunkel's song 'Bridge over Troubled Waters'. The village nestles beside the River Exe and a mill was recorded in the Domesday survey although the present mill only dates from the 18th century. Corn was ground here until the 1950s and soon afterwards it fell into disrepair, but was restored and opened to the public as a craft centre in 1973. It is open from 10 am to 6 pm every day between April and October. In November and December it closes at 5 pm. Between January and March the centre only opens on Saturdays and Sundays. It is pleasant to see that dogs on leads are welcome.

Whatever your interest in the country-scene may be, there is something at the Devonshire Centre for you. There is a working 19th-century farm using shire horses and human muscle as its source of power rather than machines. Photographers love this area with its collection of rare breeds of cattle, sheep, pigs, goats and poultry. If you fancy trying to milk a cow you may well get the chance. A waterwheel which once drove a mill in Dulverton still works although these days it is not connected to wheels grinding corn. There is a demonstration of the process of milling and in the same building other crafts are seen including potting and spinning.

Crediton Church, one of the oldest in Devon, is of cathedral-like proportions.

A large pond has been surrounded by viewing platforms from which rainbow trout can be observed and it is possible to hire a fly-fishing rod and a tutor. Another pond has been scraped out to provide a habitat for exotic birds including flamingoes, wildfowl and penguins. There is a leisure area and a picnic centre close to which is an island on which short-clawed otters are kept. These are smaller than the British species, but they are just as poetic when swimming in the water.

There is a fine collection of veteran, vintage and collectors' motor vehicles all of which are in working condition. The Millstones' Licensed Restaurant provides food of a high standard and there is also a gift shop, farm shop and bakery.

A friend once told us that there was nothing to see at Crediton except traffic thundering through the town along the Exeter road. In one sense this is true but in another it is gross slander. Crediton would have been a beautiful town had it not been for a series of disastrous fires, the worst being in 1743 and which in ten hours killed 14 people and destroyed 460 buildings. Thus the old Saxon town once known as Kirton (Churchtown) was destroyed.

What was not destroyed, however, was the history and visitors who have the time to spare will be rewarded by a walk through the town. This should start at the Church of the Holy Cross, and with a study of the life of Winfrith who later became St. Boniface. He was born at Crediton in AD 680, but as a young boy he was sent to the Benedictine Abbey at Nursling near Southampton. He proved to be so able that on the death of his abbot in AD 716 he was offered the position, but by that time the young man was fired by a missionary zeal. Off he went to convert the heathen tribes of Frisia and then in Hesse, now part of Germany. He proved so good at this difficult and dangerous task that the Pope gave him the name Boniface which meant the 'doer of good'. In AD 722 Pope Gregory made him bishop of all Germany to the east of the Rhine and for the next 30 years Boniface did a great deal of good. His bravery was beyond dispute and he actually chopped down the sacred oak of Thor in front of the hostile tribesmen of Geismar and then managed to set up a church. In the church at Crediton these and other events in the life of Boniface are recorded in stained glass. In 738 he became Archbishop and it was Boniface who crowned Pepin the King of all the Franks in 751 and thus linked the papacy with the Franks, a union which facilitated the formation of Charlemagne's Holy Roman Empire in the 780s. On the 6th June 785, however, the heathens had their revenge and ambushed Boniface and hacked him to death. It seems he had tried to fend off a sword blow with his bible, and he is often depicted using the holy book as a shield, but it was pierced by the sword. His remains were interred at Fulda and there are still exchange visits between this German town and Crediton.

It was probably because of Boniface that Crediton was at first chosen as the religious focus of Devon in preference to Exeter. Bishop Forthere of Sherborne and Queen Frithogyth, wife of the King of Wessex, which then included Crediton, visited the Pope. There they almost certainly met Boniface and the next year – 739 – King Aethelheard, no doubt prompted by his wife, gave land to construct a monastery at Boniface's home town of 'Cridie'. The building was erected of wood and thatch and said to be dedicated to St Gregory but it did not have a peaceful evolution thanks to the marauding Danes who harassed Wessex for many years. Just before the Norman conquest Bishop Leofric petitioned the pope successfully to remove his see to Exeter where safety was provided by the substantial Roman walls which at that time still stood.

Crediton, however, had tradition and in 1150 the Normans sanctioned the building of a collegiate church and this is the basis of the present parish church which is cathedral-like in its red sandstone magnificence. The college for training priests used the tower, quire and trancepts whilst the townspeople worshipped in the main body of the church. When Henry VIII dissolved the monasteries in the 1530s Crediton had a problem – if the college was dismantled there would be no parish church. The solution was for the townspeople to pay £200 to the king for the church. After the death of Henry VIII young Edward IV granted a charter in 1547 which gave 12 elected governors of the church the power to choose their own vicar and to have all 'goods and tithes belonging to it'. This was called a 'peculiar' parish and still operates; the governors' room is furnished in the style of the 16th century.

Then there was the problem of what to do with the collegiate school first established within the 739 Saxon monastery. This was re-founded in the reign of Elizabeth I and bears her name to the present day. A new school was built in 1860 but prior to this students were taught in what is now the Lady Chapel. The old school door can still be seen although it is now blocked up, but the Lady Chapel retains its link with the young by holding children's services within its walls.

The furnishings in the church are also cathedral-like in both scale and quality. Some of the stained glass is magnificent, there is a 15th-century Flemish merchant's chest, and a fine monument celebrating the life of Sir William Perryman who died in 1650. He was one of the judges in the trial of Mary Queen of Scots and also one of the church governors. The Tuckfield monument was erected in 1630 and commemorates the life of Elizabeth, her husband and her father-in-law.

Those interested in the life of Boniface should also visit the modern Roman Catholic church dedicated to the saint. When building started in 1969 the Bishop of Fulda gave a stone from St Boniface's tomb and also some 'relics of his body'. There is also a stained glass window which depicts his life and was donated by the monks of Buckfast Abbey. Another religious house in Crediton not to be missed is the Chapel of St Lawrence built around 1200 as an anchorite cell for religious men to enjoy seclusion and prayer. During the summer a series of Saint Boniface concerts

The splendid interior of Crediton Church.

are organised within the church, and also at other venues in and around the town.

From as early as the 12th century Crediton was known for its woollen products especially a high quality serge called Kirton. Humphrey Spurway was one who made his fortune from this trade and who set up a set of four almshouses in 1555 which are occupied to the present day.

Crediton can be used as a base from which to explore surrounding villages including Cheriton Fitzpaine and Colebrooke. The former has some delightfully attractive thatched buildings and a solid 15th-century church. It is overlooked by a wooded hill from which there are long views over towards the Tors of Dartmoor. Colebrooke's church dates from the 14th and 15th centuries and it is worth the time to explore the interior which has some crudely fashioned but attractive carvings on the bench ends.

Leaving Crediton and following a winding road our car journey to Bideford took in a number of villages including Winkleigh, Monkokehampton and Holsworthy. Winkleigh was important in Saxon England and the owner just prior to the Norman invasion and during the reign of Edward the Confessor, bore the glorious name of Brictric of the Golden Hair. He was thane of Gloucester and the grandson of Lesfire the Earl of Mercia. William the Conqueror settled this area, and many others, on his wife Matilda but soon after this the manor was split into two which accounts for the two castle sites at either end of the village. These seem not to have been true castles but rather fortified manor houses set on hills and surrounded by deep moats. The two manors were known as Wynkelegh Keynes and Wynkelegh Tracey, the latter relating to the family of a knight implicated in the murder of Thomas à Becket. Castle School stands on the site of the house of this family.

There is a tradition that the church here was originally dedicated to St Thomas but it is now dedicated to All Saints. Bits of the present building date from the 12th century although the main work was fashioned in the 14th and 15th centuries. There have been many restorations since, the last in 1975, but it remains an interesting and impressive building. The view from the tower which stands 550 feet (166 m) above sea level is magnificent and it is easy to see how important the village was in the early days of organised commercial road traffic. Billings' 'County Director' of 1858 recorded, 'The village, very commandingly situated on the Exeter and Torrington turnpike road, is very healthy and has several genteel residences.'

As we strolled quietly along Castle Street and Barnstaple Street, which radiate from the unspoiled Fore Street, we were able to watch thatchers at work and felt glad that such old crafts still survive. An obelisk in the market square on Fore Street was erected in 1832 as a monument to William IV and was later adapted as a support for the village pump which still stands.

The Tuckfield monument inside Crediton Church.

In January 1991 whilst writing our outline of this chapter, we stopped for a picnic in the tiny hamlet of Monkokehampton and stumbled upon a charming piece of nostalgia which at any other time we would have missed. Secured to the wall of the blacksmith's shop was the black and gold winged crest of the AA indicating 7½ miles to Okehampton and 196 miles to London. This 1930s' sign was discovered in the blacksmith's store after having lain there since its removal at the start of the Second Word War when anything likely to help the invader was put away. It was restored by Eric Hughes of Combe Martin who retired in 1990 after 40 years' service with the AA. For the rest there is little of note within the small hamlet, but in the church, restored in 1855, is an east

The Balaclava monument, which gives thanks for the final sacrifice of a gallant officer.

window which was displayed at the 1851 Exhibition.

On the outskirts of Hatherleigh are two interesting monuments. The Balaclava monument was erected by Sir Robert White-Thomson in memory of his brother, John Henry, who fell at the battle of Balaclava on 25th October 1854; the Lieutenant was one of many members of the 17th lancers who died on that fateful day. At the crossroads at the entry to the village is an ancient cross which once guided travellers to the Hatherleigh holdings established by Tavistock Abbey in 974. In the village itself are two 15th-century inns, the George and the White Hart House, plus the national school which looks to be about the same age but which was actually built in 1838. The church is also of interest with both a Saxon and a Norman font, a waggon roof, Jacobean panelling and some impressive Flemish glass dated from 1653.

Between the lovely old villages of Highhampton and Sheepwash is a packhorse bridge of five arches spanning the River Torridge, a river which in these hilly areas can be sprightly after rain or snow melt. Fishermen staying at the Half-Moon Inn enjoy the sport and historians love the village of Sheepwash itself which still faithfully follows its original Saxon plan.

Holsworthy is a much more substantial settlement which has had a fair and a fish market since the 12th century but apart from bits of the substantial church nothing of the ancient appears to have survived the 19th-century swamping. The Parish Church of St Peter and St Paul is on the site of a Saxon church, but what would have been a thatched structure was replaced by a stone building between 1030 and 1130 with the south nave pillar and tower dating from 1430 although much alteration, some of it intensive, took place in Victorian times. The organ, however, is interesting and much travelled and still in its carved 17th-century case. It began life at All Saints Chelsea in the reign of Charles I, but in 1723 it was sold to Bideford; in 1865 it was acquired by St Peter and St Paul and it still has a sonorous and mellow tone.

Opposite the church is a large car park next to the council offices which are shared by the museum. This is open from May to September from 10 am to 4 pm and on Wednesdays only during April and October. It is run by volunteers and there is a nominal entry fee. The museum is housed in a 17th-century manor house which in 1724 was bought by the Bishop of Exeter who used it as a parsonage. Alterations were made during the Georgian period and there is evidence of both periods of architecture in the exterior appearance and interior design.

The museum collection began in the 1920s when a group of informal local antiquaries combined their own possessions and stored them above a printer's shop in Victoria Square. During the Second World War their storage space was required first by the Home Guard and then by American troops. It was only in 1967 that the collection was restored and in 1978 the present accommodation was obtained and is already groaning at the seams. The collection is wide ranging, the honorary curator a mine of information about furniture and photographs, the local

Holsworthy Station in the glorious days of steam in 1883.

canal which closed long ago and the railway which was a victim of the Beeching cuts. He showed us a breast plough driven by a farmworker pushing with his chest on the implement which stripped turf and levelled mole hills. We were also shown a clam oven which was typical of cottage fireplaces in Devon. They were pre-heated with bundles of twigs and the retained heat was used for the baking. They were marked with a specific number of carved grooves to indicate how many loaves would be produced in one baking. The museum holds hundreds of photographs including one showing cattle being driven into the market in the 1880s and a picture of the hunting and dog-breeding clergyman Jack Russell taken about the same time.

For those with time to plan a visit to Holsworthy, a Wednesday or a Thursday should be chosen when there is the hustle, bustle and banter of a cattle market, whilst there is also a vibrant street market on Wednesdays. St Peter's Fair Day is held in July when the town crier raises his voice over the clamour to celebrate 'Ye charter to open ye fayre and witness the Pretty Maid ceremony at twelve o'clock.'

Another drive along narrow roads and between high hedges ends in a surprise as the descent into Great-Torrington reveals substantial industry along the valley of the River Torridge overlooked by Castle Hill. This is a good place to start a tour of the town although the castle has long gone with a bowling green now occupying its former site. The best route is through the pannier market of 1842, the entrance to which is now occupied by the county library. A row of market booths is still in use and gives a feel of an old country town long since lost to most of England. The church only dates from 1651, thanks to the tragic event during the Civil War. In 1645 St Michael and All Angels was blown up with around 200 Royalist prisoners still inside. They had apparently been using the church as an arsenal.

There are not many buildings of architectural note here but on New Street is Palmer House built in 1752 of red brick with Ionic palasters and a curtain wall. John Palmer married Sir Joshua Reynolds' sister and the great painter often stayed in Great Torrington as did Dr Johnson, along with his companion and biographer Boswell. The story of the town is well told in the museum situated on the square close to the information centre.

Signposted from the town centre and from many other roads in the area is the Dartington Crystal Factory on School Lane. There are organised tours where visitors can watch glass being blown and crafted; there is a reconstruction of an 18th-century glass cone and a collection showing the history of glassmaking. There are audiovisual displays, a factory shop and a licensed restaurant and snack bar. Here again is the chance for visitors to purchase unusual presents even if they cost that little extra which quality can always command.

Visitors to Great Torrington should not miss the Royal Horticultural Society's Rosemoor Garden situated one mile to the south-east on the B3220 road which leads towards Exeter. There is a free car park, picnic area, shop and plant sales' area which is open to non-visitors and a licensed restaurant. It is the gardens, however, which are the real joy and there are excellent facilities for the disabled. The garden is open throughout the year with the visitors' centre open every day from March 1st to December 15th.

Lady Anne Palmer created the eight acres of gardens which have such a variety of trees, shrubs, bulbs and herbaceous plants that there is colour all the year round. In 1988 Lady Anne gave Rosemoor to the Royal Horticultural Society and through the

Looking down at the old harbour of Clovelly, the old limekiln is clearly seen in the foreground.

1990s it is hoped to develop a 32-acre national garden and it is likely to be the major horticultural focus not only for Devon but for the whole of the United Kingdom.

If the gardens please the adults then the Great Torrington miniature railway delights all, especially the children, as its tough little steam locomotives carry passengers up and down a charming little valley. What wonderful memories the smell of steam brought back to us one glorious day in early August.

Between Great Torrington and Holsworthy there are signs to Tamar lakes which are ideal for those interested in water sports. From Great Torrington it is a short journey to Bideford which is a convenient place from which to explore the coast of North Devon.

Bideford and Barnstaple, sited around the estuaries of the Taw and Torridge rivers, dominate this area historically. Barnstaple will be described in the next chapter, but we will conclude this chapter at Bideford which serves as a base from which to explore the Hartland peninsula and Clovelly, Westward Ho, Appledore and Northam Burrows Country Park.

Henry Williamson describes Tarka the otter swimming under the 24-arched Bideford Bridge which was built around 1460 and which we feel is one of the most imposing bridges in an area so full of impressive spans of all shapes and sizes. The River Torridge flows beneath the arches and pushes against the timbers of vessels including the Lundy ferry, the M. V. *Oldenburg*, which is berthed at Bideford. This was once a major port, and despite a drastic decline in the seafaring business in recent years, it seems to have retained the atmosphere of a thriving seagoing settlement. There is good parking on the quayside near the bridge. These days Bideford relies mainly on light industry and farming whilst tourists are becoming ever more important to the economy.

From the mid-16th century to the mid-18th century was Bideford's period of glory with the Grenville family being instrumental in the granting of the town charter in 1573. Sir Richard Grenville's little ship *Revenge,* crewed by men from Bideford, gave a good account of herself in 1591 in a fight with 15 Spanish ships off the Azores. The town built many fine ships of good English oak, and was a bustling port into which flowed Newfoundland salted fish, particularly cod. Between 1700 and 1755 Bideford imported more tobacco than any other British port and in the churchyard there is the grave of a North American Indian. A surprising import was wool but this merely serves to underline how active the Devon weavers were, as local production could not keep pace with demand. Much of the finished fabric was exported. Bideford at these times was prosperous, influential and busy. It is still busy and we love to stroll along the quayside people-watching or focusing our binoculars on the assortment of birds which frequent the estuary. In winter the birds outnumber the people, but at the height of the season the reverse is true and parking can be a problem.

From the harbour a short stroll leads to Bridgeland which is dominated by the substantial dwellings of the rich merchants built towards the end of the 17th century. Close to the bridge which was widened in 1925 and substantially strengthened in 1968 are the municipal buildings in which is situated a comprehensive local history museum. The Church of St Mary was substantially restored – almost rebuilt in fact – in 1865 and little remains of its Norman foundation except for a font. It is a pity that so little remains to link the church with the Elizabethan sailors.

At the north end of the quay is Victoria Park, its bandstand surrounded by a battery of cannons said to have formed the

Clovelly Harbour still has a feel of old England about it.

armaments of Spanish Armada warships. Nearby is a very good art gallery which is always popular on wet days. The view across the river reveals another merchant's house built in 1688 but now a hotel. It is said that Charles Kingsley wrote part of *Westward Ho!*, published in 1855, whilst staying at the Royal.

Bideford is an ideal place from which to explore the Hartland Peninsula, at the gateway to which stands Clovelly which describes itself as 'one of the world's unique villages'. Although this title seems a little incongruous we know what is meant. On a busy summer's day it can be impossible, but its beauty is indeed unrivalled. The steep street, often described as a waterfall of buildings, leads to the restored harbour which dates from the 14th century. Boat trips are now available and from the sea it is easy to realise how the houses were built into the hillside to achieve maximum shelter, and also to understand why Clovelly's fishing industry developed. Charles Kingsley's father was rector of Clovelly and it was the publication of *Westward Ho!* which brought in floods of tourists and made it Britain's most visited village. Credit for preserving the settlement, however, must be given to the lords of the manor, the Hamlyn family, who came to Clovelly Court in 1738. The Court and the village are still privately owned and the presence of the Clovelly Centre has proved to be a necessary intrusion. This is at the top of the hill and was opened in 1988 and the entrance fee covers parking, the use of all the facilities which includes an audiovisual presentation and there are good arrangements for the disabled. There is also a restaurant, a picnic spot and a gift shop. We have seen many folk past the first flush of youth look down towards the harbour, regret that no cars are allowed down, and drive away not having seen the real beauty of the spot. There is now an hourly land rover service for the return journey from the harbour so there is no excuse for missing the beauty and the bustle of Clovelly.

Three attractions in the Clovelly – Bideford area are 'The Milky Way', 'The Big Sheep' and occasionally Hartland Abbey. 'The Milky Way' is open every day except Saturday from Easter to the end of October and here you can try your hand at feeding lambs, calves, or kids and even learn to milk a cow. It is a 25-acre dairy farm with some of its buildings being 300-years-old. There is a museum section including a Victorian kitchen complete with a bath in front of a fire. There are also vintage cars, even older horse-drawn vehicles and an assortment of farm machinery. The owners suggest that at least three hours are allowed for the visit and we think this is a conservative estimate. Delicious cream teas are served in the thatched milk bar restaurant and there is also a well-stocked gift shop.

'The Big Sheep' opens every day from Easter to the end of October from 10 am to 6 pm and features a sheep dairy underlining the value of ewes' milk. It is situated in the village of Abbotsham near Bideford.

Hartland Abbey was built in 1160 and dissolved in 1539 since which time it has been privately owned. The Abbey was in fact the last in the country to be dissolved and was given by Henry VIII to the sergeant of his wine cellar who was aptly named William Abbot and has been passed down to his relatives, by blood or marriage, ever since. It is open from 2 pm to 5 pm each Wednesday between May and September plus the Sundays and Mondays of bank holidays. It also opens on Sundays between July and mid-September. The gardens are a delight and there is also some furniture and porcelain. There is a display of manuscripts dating from 1160.

The rest of Hartland Peninsula has more beauty and less bustle and for this reason is highly regarded as walking country although Hartland Quay and Coastal Museum are developing and during

Passengers landed by rowing boat from the paddle steamer seldom reached Clovelly Harbour without getting splashed.

the 1990s are likely to become a major attraction. The museum is open daily from 11 am to 5 pm during Easter week and from Whitsuntide until the end of September. Hartland Quay is the site of a port, dating at least from the 16th century, a haven amongst awe-inspiring coastal scenery as savage and treacherous as any in the world. No wonder that this was a centre of shipwrecking and smuggling, both of which are described and graphically illustrated in the museum. In the summer is a marine aquarium and lighthouse which can be visited and reflecst the more pleasant side of Hartland. The old customs house and ware-houses are now combined to form a family hotel which serves substantial bar snacks. The views over the rough and dangerous seas to steep cliffs marked with fault lines are spectacular and gulls and fulmars nest on narrow ledges.

This maritime theme is continued at Appledore which is also easily reached from Bideford. There is good parking along the quayside, but also close to the Maritime Museum. This was the 19th-century home of merchants, ship owners and their sea captains. It is open from Easter to the end of October each afternoon from 2 pm to 5 pm. From Spring Bank Holiday until the end of September it is also open on weekday mornings between 11 am and 1 pm. One room explains the link between

Appledore and Prince Edward Island off the coast of Canada in the 19th century. A timber shortage in Europe persuaded the shipbuilders to construct vessels on the island and then sail them back to Appledore to have the final touches added by the skilled workers based at Richmond dock.

The whole of Appledore is a museum in its own right and we never tire of walking its narrow streets making lists of cottage names including Smuggler's Run, Crab Quay and Cockle Cottage. We also enjoy our winter visits to the modern St Mary's Church. In the cemetery grows butterbur which in January adds its sweet perfume to the ozone-rich air and anticipates spring. Down on the quayside the smell of rope, oil and fish combine to prove that Appledore is not just a tourist trap but still a hard working port. Shipbuilding still survives and produces trawlers and naval vessels, but also replicas of historic wooden ships including the Hudson Bay Company's *Nonsuch* of the 17th century and also Sir Frances Drake's *Golden Hinde.* Also on the historic list are Viking longship and a Roman galley. The modern vessels are built in Europe's largest covered yard.

In the summer Appledore is a favourite anchorage for pleasure cruisers and yachts whilst there are boats for hire and a ferry plies across the river to Instow, an increasingly popular holiday resort.

A 1930s view of the bridge over the Torridge at Bideford. It is much busier these days.

Its little harbour is an ideal place from which to watch the annual Appledore regatta which is held in late July or early August.

Westward Ho!, contrary to popular opinion is not an ancient settlement but of recent date being founded in 1806 and taking its name from Charles Kingsley's novel. Although it was built as a rival to Torquay it never quite achieved its aim although there is no arguing that from a distance it is pretty, with stately Victorian dwellings overlooking the bay. In 1874 some of these houses were converted into the United Services College where the sons of officers were educated whilst their fathers were away fighting for the Empire. In the early 1900s it was closed, the school being amalgamated with Haileybury and this would have been the end of it had it not been for an ex-pupil by the name of Rudyard Kipling. He based his novel *Stalky and Co* on the school and the area.

Westward Ho! is seen at its best from Northam Burrows which shelters behind a 1½-mile-long barrier of shingle beyond which is a splendid stretch of open beach. This is safe and ideal for surfing and sailboarding. The 640-acre grassy coastal plain has lots of good parking and visitors get the chance to see the sheep and cattle which belong to the Potwallopers of Northam. These are the people who still retain the ancient common rights of pasture.

The Burrows' Centre is located at Sandymore and is open daily from Easter to the end of September from 10 am to 5 pm but the country park is open all day every day. At the centre are toilets, a souvenir shop plus an exhibition and activity area. The centre and the toilets have ramps for the disabled. Nearby there is also an 18-hole golf course and horses are available for hire at local riding stables.

The Burrows have been given the status of a Site of Special Scientific Interest (S.S.S.I.) and a leaflet is available. The wildlife here can be spectacular and can rival that at Braunton Burrows, near Barnstaple, which is described in the next chapter.

CHAPTER 5

Barnstaple and Devonia

Any town is seen at its best on market day, and Barnstaple has three held on Tuesday, Friday and Saturday. It is the ideal centre from which to tour the resorts of Braunton, Saunton Sands, Croyde, Woolacombe and Morthoe, not forgetting Ilfracombe, which is another ideal base from which to launch a coastal journey through Devonia.

Barnstaple has two irresistible attractions – history and energy. Here is one of the oldest boroughs in Britain and it was, like Watchet, to be described in Chapter 11, minting its own coins during the 10th century. Following the Norman conquest Barnstaple evolved as a textile and shipbuilding centre and held a dominant position during the reign of Queen Elizabeth I (1558-1603). Its 16-arched bridge was first built of stone around 1437, but has been strengthened and altered several times since and easily handles the busy traffic streaming across the River Taw. Although its initial trades have declined substantially in recent years it is still the largest town in North Devon and an important site of agricultural and light industry. Its textile industry declined during the 17th century, whilst shipbuilding did not finally cease until around 1880. This demise was partly due to iron steamships replacing the wooden sailing vessels and partly because the Taw estuary had gradually silted up to such an extent that large ships could no longer reach the harbour. Barnstaple has also a tradition of producing fine pottery and on the road out of town signposted Bude is the Royal Barum Pottery which has a fine visitors' centre, museum and a well-stocked shop.

To discover the energy of Barnstaple a Friday visit to the Pannier Market is required. Following the building of the Guildhall in 1827 the council undertook a major redevelopment and by 1855 the scheme was completed with the Pannier Market, which looks rather like a high glass-roofed Victorian railway station, the focus of the scheme. Also built next to the market was a row of 33 small shops known as Butcher's Row which still operates to this day. For local folk and for those taking self-

The Pannier Market at Barnstaple.

catering holidays, there is no better place to shop. Before the construction of the market, farmers and tradesmen walked into town carrying their wares in large baskets called panniers. The new market protected the vendors and their produce from the elements. The sound, sight and smell of the place produces a unique atmosphere. Footsteps and voices echo from the glass and iron roof, greengrocers lay out their wares with stalls selling old records, pictures and books on one side of them and those specialising in Devon cream and delicious fudge on the other; and then there are the blended scents of cabbage and coffee, butter and bananas, soap and sweets, leather and lemons, flowers and footwear, pears and pate plus many other aromas difficult to name. This market is spectacular itself and it comes as something of a pleasant surprise to find that special events are organised on

Bee – otter and star of television.

the first Saturday in March, April, May, June, October, November and December. During the four-day fair held in September the market also plays its colourful part.

The best way to leave the market area is by passing along the narrow alleys between the butchers' shops leading to the library and information centre. Each Friday a cattle market is held nearby. Beyond this modern complex of buildings is the ancient mound called Castle Hill. There is evidence that a motte and bailey was here in the 12th century probably on the site of a Saxon hill fort guarding a ford across the river and therefore controlling the area.

St. Mary's Parish Church has some 14th-century parts remaining, the timber-framed lead-lined spire was built in the 17th century, and inside are some beautifully fashioned wall monuments. Even older than the parish church is St. Anne's Chapel built in the early 14th century. Although it is not used for worship now it functions as an informative museum. Barnstaple has a good museum service and the new Museum of North Devon is set to develop quickly during the 1990s and has recently taken over a rather fine Victorian building. The intention is to co-ordinate St. Anne's Chapel Museum, founded in 1928, with the collection of the Barnstaple Literary and Scientific Institution which dates back to 1845 plus that of the Devon Athenaeum founded in 1880. The new museum is open throughout the year between Tuesday and Saturday from 10 am to 4.30 pm and entry is free. The collections include archaeology, natural history (the fern collection is particularly good), pottery for which the area has long been famous and the Royal Devon yeomanry are also honoured here.

No visitors to Barnstaple should miss Queen Anne's Walk which was first constructed in 1609 but rebuilt about a century later. It is an attractive little arcade dominated by a statue of Queen Anne, the last of the Stuart monarchs. Other historic buildings include the Three Tuns Inn opposite the Guild Hall and despite several alterations much of its 15th-century structure remains. The National Westminster Bank with its fine plaster ceiling and the Royal and Fortescue Hotel are both good examples of the 17th-century architecture, as are a set of almshouses near St. Anne's Chapel. It is, however, people as much as buildings which give historic towns their character.

Famous men with local connections include James Wilson, a sea captain captured by the Spaniards, but who refused to act as a navigator to the Armada Fleet, Sir Francis Chichester, the world's greatest yatchtsman during the 1960s and 70s and John Gay who was born in Barnstaple in 1685 and who composed *The Beggars Opera.* Last but not least we have Henry Williamson the author or *Tarka the Otter* who set his story around the rivers Taw and Torridge.

During the 1990s the Tarka Trail is set to become a major tourist attraction. When it was published in 1927 Tarka was an immediate success but most people thought it was just a lovely fictional story. Williamson, however, based his tale on real locations and these still exist. During the spring of 1991 we wrote and presented a short television film for children about the Tarka Trail. We used a lovely little short-clawed otter named Bee who behaved perfectly, prompted by her owner. Eventually a long distance walk of about 180 miles (290 km) will be marked and should be complete by the late 1990s although a considerable stretch is already in operation. The idea is to produce a figure-of-eight circuit based on Barnstaple. The northern circuit takes in Exmoor and the North Devon coast and this is already walkable as it follows sections of footpaths already open, namely the Two Moors' Way and the South-West Coast Path. There is a Tarka Trail cycle hire service based at Barnstaple railway station where

The otter in its normal habitat. The European otter is still a feature of Devon's rivers.

there is also a museum concerned with the now defunct Lynton to Barnstaple narrow gauge railway which is described in Chapter 7. In January and February the cycle hire centre is closed but it is open at weekends in March, April, November and December. It is open every day from May to October from 9 am to 5 pm. A range of cycles is available both for adults and children and there are also tandems and adult tricycles which are ideal for the disabled. There are usually enough cycles to meet demand but at peak times it is as well to book by telephone (Barnstaple 24202).

For those who explore by car there is a splendid coastal route to Ilfracombe which takes in a number of resorts collectively known as Devonia. The A361 is taken to Braunton and then the B3231 is followed through Saunton, Croyde and Georgeham where Henry Williamson lived and then on to Woolacombe, Mortehoe and Lee Bay to Ilfracombe.

We are never sure whether Braunton is a town or a village but the authorities have played safe by pointing out that it is the largest village in England. There has been a religious focus since the 6th century and a Welsh missionary, St. Brannock, established a chapel. Legend has it that a suitable site was revealed to him in a dream which told him to build on the spot where he found a sow with a litter of pigs. The present church is almost certainly on the same site and dates mainly from the 13th century. The 16th-century bench ends are so exquisitely carved that they are regarded as amongst the finest in the country. One of the roof bosses depicts a sow with her litter thus linking with the legend of St. Brannock. The village itself is a sprawl of modern streets interspersed with ancient cottages which makes its history hard to unravel without help. This is available at the Braunton and district museum which is evolving into one of the best in the area, now open regularly during the tourist season, and always open on summer Tuesdays and Saturdays and should not be missed. Exhibitions deal with local crafts and history plus good coverage of the fishing and farming industries. The latter is particularly interesting because just outside the village a valuable piece of agricultural history can still be seen. Braunton Great Field is an example of the medieval open field method of cultivation with its 350 acres (140 hectares) divided into strips and it was once divided among the villagers. Such systems were destroyed when the Enclosure Acts resulted in developments of farms with large fields owned by one person and kept private by the construction of hedges.

Our visits to Braunton are usually well planned and eagerly anticipated. The museum is developing all the time and there is always something new to see, after which we collect our lunch from one of several good fish and chip shops in the village. We then drive past the Great Field and on down a narrow side road signposted Braunton Burrows, surely one of the best nature reserves in Britain and where there is ample parking in the shelter of a huge sand dune system. The area is over a mile wide and more than four miles long – no wonder botanists love it. Attractive guide booklets to the area can be purchased from Braunton museum. On the Burrows grows sea holly which was used in Shakespeare's time as a sweet called eringo and which is mentioned in *The Merry Wives of Windsor* as being a favourite of Sir John Falstaff. Other species include stonecrop, stork's-bill and our favourite the sea bindweed with its trumpet-shaped flowers delicately coloured pink. Between May and the end of

Two plants common on the Burrows are the sea holly and the sea bindweed.

August the damp areas called dune slacks are also a mass of flowers such as marsh orchid, common twayblade, hemp agrimony, yellow iris, whilst in the drier areas grow viper's bugloss, thyme, Portland and sea spurge plus strinking iris and hound's tongue which has a distinct smell of mice.

Beyond the dunes is an open area of sandy beach, an ideal place for seeking shells including those of the pink tellin, mussel and the common whelk. In winter Braunton Burrows can be an exciting place to bird watch with redshank, curlew, lapwing and oyster catcher all being common but in really cold weather the patient watcher may be rewarded by a sighting of a shore lark. There is only one drawback to the area and that is the proximity of low flying aircraft from RAF Chivenor and its occasional use by the armed forces, their presence signalled by the flying of red flags. The locals still refer to the lane leading to the reserve as American road as the GIs trained here in preparation for the Normandy landings.

Braunton reminds us of parts of Norfolk with its flat windswept areas, and further along the coast Saunton Sands feels very like one of Jersey's magnificent bays. It would be more accurate to say that the glory of Devonia lies in its bewildering variety of scenery. Saunton is sheltered by Braunton Burrows but its vast area of sand is popular with holiday-makers. There is a grand walk along the sand to Crow Point where the waters of the Taw and the Torridge meet the Atlantic swell, a combination which produces a perfect place for surfing, although swimmers need to take great care, especially at the southern end of the bay.

Just inland from Saunton are the thatched, colour-washed cottages of Croyde from which a path leads down to the sea. Croyde to us means two things, the best ice cream in the world, served with a generous helping of Devon cream and secondly the gem-rock museum. Exhibits here include giant clams from the Pacific as well as European species and there is also the chance to see semi-precious stones being cut into jewellery some of which are on sale. The museum is open every day from March to the end of October between 10 am and 5.30 pm and in July and August from 10 am to 10 pm. There is winter opening by appointment. Exmoor and North Devon in addition to beautiful scenery provide more opportunities than most holiday areas to find unusual holiday presents at a price to suit all pockets.

Around two miles to the north-east of Croyde is the solid stone village of Georgeham which takes its name from the patron saint of the church which has a dominating 14th-century tower. The steep narrow winding street would have been well known to Henry Williamson who spent most of his life in Georgeham.

It is possible to walk to Ilfracombe along a coastal path with the three villages of Croyde, Mortehoe and Woolacombe all having fine beaches sheltered by the two dramatic headlands of Morte and Baggy Points. There are also small secluded bays at Rockham, Grunta and Combesgate which all have deep, safe rock pools which are a joy to naturalists in search of sea urchins, butterfish, sea anemones and the occasional starfish. Close to Mortehoe is Barricane Beach which is made up of small sea shells not native to Britain but carried from the tropical waters of the Caribbean by the ocean currents. Seen on a hot summer's day with blue sky and a gentle breeze, both Woolacombe and Mortehoe itself are serious rivals to the West Indies.

The road down into Woolacombe is steep, with the hillside swamped beneath so many new hotels that it has a distinct feel of the Spanish 'Costas' about it, but once on the beach its popularity is easily understood. A narrow road climbs onto a headland dominated by gorse to the longest car park we have ever seen with each car guaranteed a delightful view and with a number of explanatory notice boards. In summer this is picnic and sunbathing country, but whatever the weather this is naturalists' country with linnet, meadow pipit and stonechat always present. When Woolacombe is busy a walk to nearby Putsborough Sand is usually quiet and there is a safe bathing beach. Woolacombe is a relatively modern settlement developing in tune with the demands of visitors to Devonia. Mortehoe is a much more ancient settlement set on a steep hill overlooking Woolacombe and dominated by its 13th-century church. St. Mary's is said to have been founded by a priest named William de Tracey and it is one of the unspoiled churches of which Devon has a goodly number. There is a set of 16th-century bench ends on which are carved coats of arms, the instrument of the passion, and a set of fearsome-looking sea monsters. From the church there are any number of walks, our favourite being to the west and over the National Trust land to Morte Point. This was an infamous headland in the days of sailing ships and during the winter of

1852 five vessels were wrecked on the Morte rocks. Many others were lured to their fate during the 18th century when local wreckers waved false lights to confuse ships' masters anxiously battling with the natural elements and on the look-out for a friendly beam. Another walk of about one mile to the north of the village leads to the automatic light on Bulk Point which is still a vital navigational aid to ships in the Bristol Channel.

The whole of the Devonia coast is a delight. It has a capital town at Barnstaple. All it needs is a 'capital seaside resort' and this is the role of Ilfracombe which is described in the next chapter.

CHAPTER 6

Ilfracombe to Lynmouth

We both remember our first visits to Ilfracombe as children just after the Second World War and long before we ever met. The sun was so hot that we blistered after sitting exposed on the harbour wall watching the comings and goings of the fishing boats. We have returned many times since including a special journey during the preparation of this book which brought back such vivid memories of the searing heat all those years ago. We managed to park at the end of the harbour and watched holiday-makers sweltering under the sun which blazed down out of a clear blue August sky. Boats bobbed lazily on an equally blue sea and the M. V. *Waverley* cut a smooth white wake as she headed out of the snug little harbour carrying passengers out into the Bristol Channel.

Actually Ilfracombe harbour was officially declared a port during the reign of Henry III (1327-1377). It was granted a market and a fair in 1278 and when Edward II (1307-1327) organised an expedition to fight Robert the Bruce in Scotland, Ilfracombe made a considerable contribution of ships and seamen. The port's assistance to Edward III's siege of Calais in 1346 was even greater and involved the provision of six ships and around 100 sailors. With such an impressive history of service it was no wonder that Elizabeth was able to rely on Ilfracombe to provide transport and victuals for almost 1,000 troops. During the Civil Wars of the 1640s the harbour was the scene of skirmishes as both Royalists and Parliamentarians realised the value of the port.

Few buildings remain relating to this time as Ilfracombe was an insignificant fishing village set around an important harbour. Two ecclesiastical buildings do remain, both of which overlook the harbour. The Parish Church of Holy Trinity has been much restored since its foundation in the 13th century but fortunately its splendid waggon roof timbering has been retained. Of more interest from an ecclesiastical point of view is the ancient little chapel dedicated to St Nicholas which is set on Lantern Hill overlooking the harbour and can be reached via a steep winding

Bracing sea trips on the Balmoral are a feature of Ilfracombe in the summer.

path from the car park. It was built around 1300 and provided a light for ancient mariners in addition to being a place of worship. It is open on most days of the year and now houses a small museum of old photographs of the harbour and the town plus some interesting displays and models. Here it can be seen how the port once made a good living from fishing, particularly of herrings until the fish changed their habits and moved away from the south-west coast. One room is still plainly furnished as a chapel and the feeling of peace remains as it has done for almost 700 years. Another place to study the relationship between Ilfracombe and the sea is Lifeboat House built in 1828 where visitors can see how the saving of human life from the jaws of the angry sea is only made possible by careful pre-planning.

Ilfracombe is delightfully situated between steep cliffs and high hills including Capstone and Hillsborough, both of which are ideal for those who like their steep walks to be rewarded by spectacular views. The less energetic may prefer to lie in the sun and there are a number of small beaches and coves, or perhaps sit on a seat on the promenade overlooked by a variety of tropical plants which thrive here because of a lack of winter frosts.

The young and active need not be disappointed either as there is a good theatre, many bars, discos and dance halls plus discreetly-sited bingo halls. Ilfracombe gets more than its share of sunshine

Ilfracombe Harbour at the peak of a Victorian holiday season.

which makes the famous tunnel beaches with safe tidal pools ever popular.

If the weather is right, then a splendid day trip can be made to the Island of Lundy. The M. S. *Oldenburg* sails from Bideford throughout the year but in summer the trip from Ilfracombe is popular. The journey takes just over two hours and on board there is a buffet, bar and shop and the below-deck saloons are well appointed. Children love this trip but sensibly no dogs are allowed either on the *Oldenburg* or on the island.

Lundy is not known to many apart from references made on the shipping forecast, but set in the middle of the Bristol Channel it can be an enchanting place especially to those with a love of natural history.

Landing on the island is an excitement in itself as there is no harbour and passengers are transferred to a landing stage by small launch with the *Oldenburg's* timetable so arranged as to allow almost four hours on the island. Lundy is not small, being 3½ miles long and half a mile across, deriving its name from the Norse word *lunde* which means a puffin and *ey* which means an island. Puffin island has soaring cliffs rising sheer from the sea to a height of around 500 feet (152 metres) with ledges which not only attract puffins but also other seabirds including guillemot, razorbill, several species of gull, fulmar and rock dove all of which breed. The flora is also exciting including thrift, scurvy grass and the famous Lundy cabbage unique to the island. Mammals to be seen include grey seals which bask in the bays, sika deer, wild soay sheep which are all welcome and the black rat which once transmitted bubonic plague around Europe and is therefore not at all welcome. It is, however, rather attractive to look at and its pelt was once much in demand to produce clothing.

About 20 people live permanently on the island which caters for tourists even having its own postage stamps, whilst the Marisco Tavern sells Lundy beer which is actually brewed on the island. It also offers a wide variety of bar snacks, whilst in the same building is a shop selling Lundy souvenirs. Those wanting more information about the history of the island should visit Linhay where there is a display concerning the history, natural history and explanatory schemes for its conservation. Lundy is now owned by the National Trust but leased to the Landmark Trust.

Lundy was for many years a haven for pirates with William de Marisco and his followers terrorising the coast of 12th-century Devon until they were caught and hung, drawn and quartered, with the island then becoming the property of the Crown. Some of the governors were self-styled kings, one of the worst being Captain Salkeld who in 1610 was nothing better than a pirate who harassed traders in the Bristol Channel. There were further tales of skulduggery 15 years later when genuine Turkish pirates used the island for two weeks and then came the French who tricked the islanders into carrying a coffin onto Lundy which contained not a body but the invaders' weapons.

The 19th century, however, saw Lundy becoming prosperous as a result of a legitimate business – quarrying. Lundy granite was used in the construction of London's Victoria Embankment and the Charing Cross Hotel. At this time, Lundy was owned by the Heaven family and there can be few 'kingdoms of heaven' more attractive than Lundy. There is limited accommodation on the island and advance booking is almost always essential.

On returning to Ilfracombe more of the history and natural history of the area can be discovered by visiting the museum founded in 1932 by Mervyn Palmer, a well-known explorer who visited South America. His donation, gathered during his travels, formed the basis of a collection which was added to by people

Pleasure craft sheltering under the lee of the rocks guarding Ilfracombe Harbour.

who had spent their lives abroad and then returned to the genteel resort of Ilfracombe to retire. The natural history section is excellent and there are also displays of old maps, paintings, photographs and costumes.

We once set ourselves a whole day to explore the Ilfracombe area, finished up by staying four days and went home with a list of things yet to be seen! Sights not to be missed include Bicclescombe Park, Hele Bay, Chambercombe Manor and Watermouth Castle.

Bicclescombe Park is within Ilfracombe itself and has colourful gardens with landscaped ponds and waterfalls. There is a pet's corner, children's playground, and a boating pool whilst energetic adults are provided with crazy golf and the chance to see an 18th-century watermill, restored by the local Rotary club to full working order.

An even better mill can be seen at Hele Bay, one mile to the east of Ilfracombe and signed off the A 399 road to Combe Martin. This 18-foot-diameter overshot waterfall powers the corn mill built in 1525. Many features of a mill grinding wholemeal flour are demonstrated, the machinery is beautifully restored and its produce is for sale in the shop. The mill is open from

St Nicholas Chapel is perched on a rock above Ilfracombe Harbour.

Easter Sunday until the end of October, Monday to Friday from 10 am to 5 pm and also on Sundays from 2 pm to 5 pm. Hele Bay is one of the best sandy beaches in North Devon and there are also good facilities for boating and fishing.

Chambercombe is a 16th-century manor house situated about one mile to the south-east of Ilfracombe. As you would expect there is a resident ghost but much more solid and dependable is the Elizabethan tester bed and other furnishings plus a priest hole, whilst the house itself is pleasantly built around courtyards, usually overflowing with fuchsias. Set in a secluded valley, a manor house was mentioned on this site in the Domesday Book which probably means that it was settled in Saxon times. Chambercombe is open from Easter Sunday to the end of September from Monday to Friday from 10.30 am to 5 pm. The last tour begins at 4.30 pm. It is closed on Saturday and opens on Sunday from 2 pm to 5.30 pm with the last tour also being at 4.30 pm. Morning coffee, light lunches and cream teas are available and on suitable days these can be served in the garden. Beyond the manor there is a splendid walk through Chambercombe Woods which in the summer delights the botanist, and is popular with birdwatchers throughout the year.

The simple interior of the early 14th-century chapel of St Nicholas, Ilfracombe.

Watermouth Castle for those with young children is worth a day to itself and is described as a family entertainment centre situated around 4 miles outside Ilfracombe and close to Combe Martin. The present building dates from 1825 and overlooks one of the most beautiful bays in Devon but the historical has been replaced by the hysterical as the fun park created in the 1980s has artificially coloured waterfalls, haunted mills and dungeons which would look much at home as the setting for a ghost train, an enchanted maze and a hauntingly noisy steam carousel. With

The Pack o' Cards at Combe Martin.

all this fun on offer it is surprising indeed to find the castle does not open at all on Saturday, and the last admission is only at 4 pm although they do suggest that three hours should be allowed for a visit.

Another attraction for children is the Combe Martin Wildlife and Leisure Park at Higher Leigh Manor which opens daily from Easter to November from 10 am with the last admission being at 5 pm. The displays are set in 20 acres of gardens including Japanese layouts with many interesting trees and shrubs some of which are rare. There are also lily ponds and artificial waterfalls.

The puffin from which Lundy Island takes its name.

Its main function is said to be that of a rare monkey sanctuary, although many other animals are on display including seals, otters, wallabies, exotic birds and during the season there are displays of birds of prey conducted by a skilful falconer. Another feature to be enjoyed, particularly by children, is the largest miniature railway to be found in North Devon, which runs through an illuminated little village built on the same scale.

The animal theme is continued at Farm World at Bodestone Barton near Berrynarbour just outside Combe Martin. It is open from Easter to October from 10.30 am to 6 pm, the last admission being at 4 pm . There is a shop, café, an outdoor adventure playground, craft demonstrations plus a fine collection of farm animals including shire horses, which actually work the fields, and Shetland ponies.

In Combe Martin itself on Cross Street, adjacent to the main car park, and behind the beach is a more historically-based reminder of transport. The Motor Cycle Museum is open from the end of May to the end of September from 10 am to 6 pm and here is a touch of real nostalgia. Some of our early explorations were done on a 1000 cc Harley Davidson motor bike, with a

The parish church of Combe Martin overlooks colourful gardens.

sidecar, which was affectionately known as 'the bomb'. There is a host of good old 'bombs' here as Nortons and AJS machines are displayed against a background of old petrol pumps and vintage garage machinery. Pure nostalgia this and there is even the smell of motor oil!

Combe Martin is probably a small town rather than a village and is said to have the longest main street in England running almost two miles down towards the sea. In the Middle Ages it was famous for its lead ore and silver mines, and if we only had X-ray eyes we would be able to see the long-disused shafts running beneath the street.

One local man with his eye on more than silver was a gambler who built the house once called the King's Arms but now renamed The Pack of Cards which is exactly what it looks like. The member of the Ley family who built it was a lucky gambler since he is said to have financed the house from his winnings.

The Pack of Cards is somewhat vulgar in an attractive sort of way but one of the most majestic buildings in the area is the Parish Church of St Peter Ad Vincular where R. D. Blackmore's grandfather John was once the rector. Solidly constructed in the 15th century, the sandstone church is set on the side of a hill; its 99-feet (30.1-metre) tower is dominant Gothic architecture at its best. Inside is the only rood screen in North Devon still to have

Martinhoe Church was probably established in Saxon times.

its original panel paintings which are 15th century and therefore pre-Reformation when such excesses of religious furnishings were frowned upon.

There may have been a wooden Saxon church on this site before the Norman conquest when it was probably known as Marhuscombe. William the Conqueror gave the area to Martin of Tours and Combe Martin and Martinhoe described later in this chapter were named after him.

Looking at the modern village, especially if one is travelling towards Ilfracombe, it is easy to forget that it was once quite an important harbour sheltered by the cliffs of Little Hangman (716 feet – 218 metres) and Great Hangman (1,043 feet – 318 metres) thrusting upwards to the east. Silver and lead plus bark from local woodlands were sent to the tanneries of Bristol and thence exported whilst imports of hemp were taken to local cottages and spun into shoemakers' thread. One export which only ceased within living memory were juicy local strawberries which were loaded onto a small steamer called the *Snowflake* and taken to the market in Swansea.

Those, like us, who are interested in dramatic coastal scenery, especially investigated on foot, should travel to Lynton and Lynmouth not along the main road via Blackmoor Gate, but via the narrow, twisting and often steep minor roads calling at Hunter's Inn, Heddon's Mouth, Martinhoe, Woody Bay and Parracombe.

At first sight Hunter's Inn seems little more than an attractive

The restored limekiln at Heddon's Mouth is situated in a most beautiful valley running down to the sea from Hunters Inn.

hotel, a café and gift shop plus extensive car parking. Why is this space needed? The answer is that a well-signposted walk leads from Hunter's Inn, alongside the river and down through glorious mixed woodlands to Heddon's Mouth. Here the river flows to the sea over a heaving mass of smooth pebbles. The sea is squeezed through a gap between towering cliffs and in summer the river, the tide and the echoing sounds of nesting seabirds produce a uniquely haunting yet strangely restful sound. On the edge of the sea is a 19th-century limekiln restored to working order between 1982 and 1986. Local limestone and coal brought from South Wales were loaded in alternate layers into the bowl and heated to around 900°C. The lime so produced was spread on the fields and also used as mortar and as limewash for buildings.

Two holes called 'the eyes of the kiln' are situated away from the prevailing westerly winds and in the nearest eye to the path is a ledge on which the workers heated their food. When it became cheaper to crush the stone rather than heat it, the kiln fell into disuse and it is more than 100 years since it last functioned seriously, but how grand it is to see it so well restored.

From Heddon's Mouth footpaths run along the coast to Lynton, via Woody Bay, but those who go by car have the added

Pleasure steamers waiting for passengers at Ilfracombe around 1895.

bonus of passing another delightful little church at Martinhoe. St Martin's is mentioned in Domesday and there has thus been settlement here since Saxon times, although the present building is early Norman. At the time of the Reformation the chancel was rebuilt but the tower was left alone. The chancel, however, does show early English features especially the triplet window. Inside the church are memorials to the 17th-century Blackmore family and in the churchyard there are many gravestones marking the resting places of the Ridd family. One Lorna Doone Ridd died in 1955 at the age of 75 and was obviously named after the heroine of the book.

The car park for Woody Bay is close to the road and those who wish to enjoy the splendid scenery can follow a steep winding track. It almost became a resort of note in the early 1900s as a pier was built to attract steamers to unload tourists but the London-based owner disappeared having 'misdirected his clients' funds'. Modern day tourists should be grateful because in this unspoiled country there are a number of Bronze Age barrows near Woody Bay car park and between Woody Bay and Heddon's Mouth is a Roman fortlet overlooking the Bristol Channel which operated for about 20 years around AD 58. On the boundary between Martinhoe and Parracombe is an Iron-age hill fort. Parracombe itself is an attractive spot on the outskirts of which is one of Devon's most interesting churches,

The sun was beating down as we followed the winding track

This picture, used by kind permission of the Ilfracombe museum, was taken in 1870, before the construction of the passenger pier. It shows the steamer *Velindra* setting out from Warp House Point.

from Parracombe village to the old church now replaced by a more modern building in the village centre. A pair of buzzards hovered over a section of the old narrow-gauge railway which once ran from Barnstaple to Lynton. Swifts screamed as they circled around the sturdy tower of the church dedicated to St Petrock, a Cornish Saint who died at Bodmin on June 4th AD 564. There are four Cornish churches and eight in Devon dedicated to him and it is thought that the origins of the Parracombe church are 8th century.

One of the most interesting of the Devon churches dedicated to St Petrock is at Timberscombe near Minehead. The present building is mainly 15th century but some historians believe that the first church on the site was built in the 6th century perhaps being supervised by the saint himself. The fan-vaulted screen is a fine example of the work of Dunster carvers who were famous around 1500, and is one of only seven examples remaining. Above the original south doorway which is now blocked up is a mural painting showing King David which is thought to date from the time of the Reformation and was only discovered in 1955.

There was certainly a church in existence at Parracombe by the 11th century and the present tower dates from 1182 and the chancel was built in 1252. The interior is of great interest and is a perfect example of a simple village church of the late 18th century – pure Georgian, in fact. There is a three-decker pulpit, some box pews along with some plain benches which date from the 16th century. One pew has had a piece cut out of it to make room for a bass viol. St Petrock's is thought to have been the last church in Devon to have had an orchestra to accompany the singing prior to the introduction of an organ. This was an ideal way of involving many of the parishioners in the service, and we wonder why it died out.

St. Petrock's was declared redundant on 25th November 1969 and was the first to be so designated and supported by funds supplied from St Andrew-by-the-Wardrobe in London's Queen Victoria Street. This underlines the importance of St Petrock's which is situated close to the A39 road not far from Lynton and Lynmouth.

Anyone interested in the history of railways, however, should visit the Lynton and Barnstaple Garden Railway situated just below the church. Open daily from 10 am to 6 pm from Easter to October except Fridays the display includes a 16 mm-to-the-foot working model of the old narrow-gauge railway with bridges and models of the old engines and rolling stock. The model is set alongside the original track bed which has been maintained almost as it was since the railway closed in the 1930s.

If only the line could have been kept open what a tourist attraction it would have been to those visiting the twin resorts of Lynton and Lynmouth.

CHAPTER 7

Little Switzerland – Lynton to Porlock

We discovered North Devon and Exmoor in general and Lynton in particular by accident. Our friends, Bob and Susan Mahon bought a hotel which turned out to be a house with a history but one which also mirrored that of the area. On the North Walk, Lynton in 1870 Thomas Hewitt built a house for his cousin who became his second wife following the death of his first. The engaged couple were standing on the cliffs overlooking Lynmouth Bay when Thomas asked Fanny if she would like to have a summer house built especially to capture the view. Seeing her face light up with excitement, he marked a stone and gave it to her saying 'Wherever it lands I will build you a house'. And so it was that Hewitts' house on the Hoe was built and so fond did Sir Thomas Hewitt, a London lawyer and his family become of the house that they spent more and more time there instead of in London. Along with his friend Sir George Newnes, the publisher, Thomas Hewitt became aware of how difficult it was for visitors to reach Lynton from London and also of the problems involved transporting goods landed at the harbour in Lynmouth to the hilltop settlement of Lynton. The two men had the answer – two railways, one to lift a carriage up the cliff and the other to connect Lynton with Barnstaple, from which there was an easy link to London. They solved both problems but, alas, only the cliff railway survives.

At one time old Mrs Arnold used to sit by the Lyndale Hotel in Lynmouth hiring ponies and donkeys to carry visitors up the hill to Lynton. An extract from *The Life of Sir George Newnes* by Hulda Friederichs, published by Hodder and Stoughton in 1911, shows how Sir Thomas Hewitt introduced Sir George to Lynton.

Sir Thomas occasionally spoke of his Devonshire home, and in return had to listen to a good deal of chaff as to his affection for a place eight hours by train from London. As if there were not plenty of country districts just as pleasant and beautiful as Lynton which it took a whole day's tiresome train journey to reach!

'Shortly after Lady Newnes and Lady Hewitt had also met and become

Wild goat grazing in the Valley of the Rocks.

friends, Sir George and his family were invited to spend a few weeks in summer with Sir Thomas and Lady Hewitt at their Devonshire home. This was before the days of motor-cars, and from Barnstaple, Lynton could only be reached by coach or private carriage; the journey uphill and down dale being long and not altogether pleasant to any one with a spark of imagination and pity. For the hills were lengthy and very steep, and the sight of the horses toiling painfully up, and struggling down with almost equal difficulty, would go a long way to spoil the traveller's pleasure in the beauty of the scenery.

'Sir George, who had a perfect horror of cruelty to any living thing, especially to creatures so helpless as an animal in the service of man, was not too favourably impressed with the long drive from Barnstaple to Lynton, although his host had thoughtfully provided two extra horses to draw the carriage up the last steep hill leading to his house.

'At the moment when these horses came in sight the travellers were just watching from their carriage another horse being forced down towards a rushing river by the too heavy load of trippers behind it; and what would have happened to this party had not a thick wall stopped them on their road to ruin, it is not pleasant to contemplate.

Hewitt's House became a hotel in 1953 and here are its first visitors.

'"Has it ever occurred to you," he asked his host, "that this river which rolls down like a torrent might be harnessed and made to bring up every ton of coal and every passenger from Lynmouth to Lynton, without any cruelty to the poor, labouring beasts, and any danger to human life?" Yes, said Sir Thomas, the idea had often been considered, but for one reason or another it had never been definitely taken up. He himself was fully persuaded that a cliff railway, worked by water-power would be an immense boon to the place.'

As early as 1870, Bob Jones, who had built The Hoe for Sir Thomas, had worked out a scheme for a cliff railway and the two of them had often discussed the subject. Bob Jones was an amazingly capable man. In his early days he emigrated to Australia in a sailing ship but he returned to Lynton after four years. He was the senior partner of the building firm of Jones Brothers and an engineer who had patented many devices and the idea of building a railway up the cliff fascinated him. The only problem was finance but Sir George had made a lot of money from publishing *Tit Bits*, *The Pall Mall Gazette*, and especially *The Strand Magazine* which began in 1891 and in which the Sherlock Holmes

The opening of the Lynton to Barnstaple Railway. Sir Thomas Hewitt is the bearded figure back centre and right of the gaslamp.

stories first appeared. He immediately offered to find the money to construct the cliff railway.

The site that was chosen was in a cleft in the rocks alongside Sir Thomas's property and it is likely that the land was given by him. He became a director and he and Sir George saw the work to a successful conclusion. It was opened on Easter Monday, 1890, when the people of the two villages enjoyed themselves riding up and down. The Lynton Cliff Railway was the first of its kind in England. It is 900-feet long with a gradient of one in one and three quarters, and rises to a vertical height of nearly 450 feet. The cars were provided with abundant safeguards in hydraulic and emergency brakes, which prevented too high a speed, and could check movement in two inches. The tanks of each car contained about three tons' weight of water, approximately 700 gallons. Its success can be judged from the fact that it has never been the subject of an accident.

The Cliff Railway was a boon to the twin villages and they quickly renamed it among themselves as 'The Lift'. It not only brought people up and down but coal and supplies arriving by

The Valley of the Rocks is the now dry valley of a river and was ground out by a glacier.

sea. The whole car was made to slide off the platform on which it was placed so as to be able to load heavy merchandise or carts. The owners of motor cars were also happy to put them on the lift rather than risk losing control when driving down the dangerous hill as had so often happened in the past.

Let us now consider the biggest undertaking of all. The Lynton and Barnstaple Railway. The train was the modern method of transport in the middle of the 19th century. The Great Western had constructed a line from Paddington to Bristol in 1841 and the North Devon had brought people as far as Barnstaple. Lynton and Lynmouth were isolated as no other area at that time and this cut them off from the prosperity which was coming with the railways.

The first meeting of the board of the new company was held on 28th June, 1895, the day after the bill received the Royal Assent. Sir George Newnes was appointed Chairman, with Sir Thomas Hewitt, Mr E. B. Jeune and Mr W. H. Halliday as directors. On May 11th, 1898, the railway was opened by Lady Newnes.

The costs of the operation had risen again and again and everyone had invested more and more money in it, convinced that the well-being of Lynton and Lynmouth depended on it. When George Newnes died in 1910 he was succeeded by Sir

The cliff railway at Lynton.

Thomas Hewitt who remained as Chairman for nine years. It was during this time that they managed to pay their first dividends, even though it was just half of one %. It had been hard, worrying work to keep the line going during the war and he was, no doubt, glad to hand over to the last of the founding directors, Col. E. B. Jeune. Sir Thomas was, after all, in his eighty-third year.

Sadly the few cars that had come to Lynton in the past became a great stream, and then came the motor bus. New roads were made for them and the Lynton and Barnstaple railway could not compete. It closed in 1935. If only we had it now, what a wonderful attraction it would be to visitors. Already there is an association with the aim of reinstating part of the line and there is great rejoicing when pieces of the old equipment are discovered. The old Barnstaple Town station is transformed into a restaurant and the signal box has been made into a museum to keep the railway's memory fresh. This is why enterprises such as the one at Bratton Fleming to set up the Exmoor Railway is a welcome link with the past.

It is still possible to find traces of the old route which wound its way around the contours from Lynton, where the old station is now a private house, via Caffyn's Halt, Woody Bay, Parracombe Halt, Blackmoor Gate where the station is now a hotel, Bratton

This card posted in 1910 shows Lynmouth long before it was devastated by floods in 1952.

Fleming, Chelfham, Snapper Halt and Barnstaple Town.

There can be no doubt that the twin villages' potential as holiday centres was initiated by the railway although literary men such as Shelley, Southey, Wordsworth and Coleridge all made the journey by road to enjoy the scenery. Nowadays the hotels are full in season, but perhaps many tourists miss the off-season attractions of magnificent and well-signposted walks to the Valley of the Rocks, the Lyn Gorge, Watersmeet and Countisbury Hill. There is also a good museum in Lynton plus the Exmoor Brass Rubbing Centre.

It is impossible these days to visit the area without seeing photographic evidence of the Lynmouth disaster. On the night of 15th August 1952 came a terrifying wind and a torrent of rain caused the East and West Lyn rivers which meet at Lynmouth to deliver an horrendous blow. A wall of water struck the village, demolishing hotels and cottages, crushing 120 cars and carrying a further 38 out to sea along with 19 boats which had been anchored in the harbour. More important than all this was the loss of 34 lives. The village was jig-sawed back together again, incorporating barriers to provide protection for the future, which have now settled into the landscape and do not disturb the old world charm which was so typical of the pre-flood village.

The Glen Lyn Gorge at Lynmouth – one of the scenic delights of North Devon.

The rugged rocks in the Valley of the Rocks and from which the area takes its name were not Druids' temples as was once suggested but were caused by weathering and erosion by rain, wind and ice. The valley itself was probably the old bed of the Lyn river before coastal erosion broke into the valley and opened up Lynmouth. The tors, as the rock formations are called, have been named Castle Rock, Rugged Jack, Chimney Rock and the Devil's Cheese Ring, obviously because of their shape.

Castle Rock is 120 metres (400 feet) above the sea and a gap in this rock looks like a lady carrying a shopping basket. A local legend grew up about the White Lady who at the time of the Crusades was badly treated by the Black Abbot of Lynton, and returned to haunt the area after her death. The valley is not short of angry females and it was said that Aggie Norman lived in a cave under Castle Rock. R. D. Blackmore used Aggie as a model on which to build his character Mother Meldrum. Chimney Rock also has evil overtones as it was often illuminated by 18th-century wreckers to lure ships carrying valuable cargo onto the rocks.

This part of the coast is the home of a herd of goats which demonstrate just how sure footed they can be. The Valley of the Rocks lies on the coastal path and it is possible to walk to Woody Bay passing Lee Abbey on the way. There is also a toll road which

St Dubricus Church at Porlock.

enables motorists to follow the line of the coast. Actually Lee Abbey is not a religious foundation although its modern usage is decidedly Christian. It was built in 1850 and is now a conference and study centre run by the Anglican Church. It is built on the site of a farmhouse owned by the De Wichehalses and which Blackmore used as one of his settings in *Lorna Doone.*

Lynmouth is not sea-bathing country and there is no sandy beach between the village and Minehead, but it is certainly river country. There are two excellent walks including the Lyn gorge, for which a small fee must be paid to follow the West Lyn, and the Watersmeet footpath which is owned by the National Trust and

Pleasure vessels sheltering in the harbour at Porlock Weir.

The Lynton to Barnstaple narrow-gauge railway descends through woodlands around Chelfham. The line closed on 29 September 1935. What a tourist attraction it would be if it was still running today.

to which there is free access at all times. Both these areas were described in great detail by Henry Williamson in *Tarka the Otter.*

Watersmeet refers to the junction of the East Lyn with Hoar Oak Water and there is a refreshment house situated here. Permits to fish the Watersmeet can be obtained from local shops and the salmon (season 1st March to 30th October) and trout (15th March to 30th September) sport is excellent.

Before leaving Lynton a visit to the Exmoor Museum is to be recommended and it is a pity that it is only open during the holiday season because it reflects life on the moor over many centuries and at all seasons. The town hall which is also open to the public and houses the information centre is a rather splendid little building given to the town by George Newnes. It was opened by Sir Arthur Conan Doyle.

The Exmoor Brass Rubbing and Hobby Craft Centre began its life in Lynton but in 1988 moved to more extensive premises down the hill in Lynmouth. There are good facilities for the disabled and young people are welcome as the centre hosts many

You can't have glorious green countryside without rain and Exmoor villages such as Winsford look pretty even in the rain, and the sound of the brook at the ford to the right makes getting wet worth it!

school visits. Entry is free, but you pay for any rubbings you actually do and there is a wide choice copied from churches all over Britain. Many materials are on sale in the shop, which also sells perfume, wooden gifts and corn dollies. The variety of crafts is being increased all the time.

The A39 road connects Lynmouth and Porlock with some interesting places both to left and right. To the right of the road is Lorna Doone country which is described in the next chapter, whilst to the left is Countisbury Hill and Culbone Church which is best reached from Porlock Weir.

The best site from which to explore Countisbury is from the Exmoor Sandpiper Inn, once called the Blue Boar and then the Blue Bell. If we could pass a law it would be to protect our pub names which are just as much a part of our heritage as are churches or castles. Countisbury, in which hamlet the old coaching inn stands, is of ancient lineage, but it is not now such a vital spot as in days of yore. The Church of St John the Evangelist close to the inn car park is a real example of 'do-it-yourself architecture'. There was a Saxon church on the site but this was replaced by a Norman structure which by 1796 had itself become dilapidated.

The Coastal Path, like the rest of Exmoor, welcomes dogs brought by considerate owners.

The locals rebuilt the nave dispensing with the services of architects and in 1836 they met again this time to construct a new tower.

The name Countisbury means 'the camp on the headland' and a breezy footpath beyond the church leads to a promontory on which stood an Iron-age fort but which later played a prominent part in Saxon history as depicted in Asser's *Life of King Alfred* and *The Anglo-Saxon Chronicle.*

Typical Devonian thatched cottage at Porlock.

In AD 878 Hubba the Dane sailed with his fleet of 23 ships from South Wales and aimed to do damage to Exmoor then ruled by King Alfred. Ealdorman Odda led the Saxons' defending forces who were in a stronghold called *Arx Cynuit* and as the water supply here was limited the Dane was confident of a victory even though it might take time. The defenders, however, did not obey the rules but charged down the hill and slaughtered 800 of the enemy including Hubba himself. The Saxons even achieved the very rare distinction of capturing the Danish raven banner. The precise location of this bloody battle has long been in dispute, but most historians are now convinced that Countisbury Castle was the place. Nearby Barna Burrow is evidence of an even older Bronze-age settlement and there was also a Roman observation fort here proving that the headland has been a vital communications link for many centuries.

The path leads onwards to Foreland Point which is the most northerly point in Devon and its sea cliffs are almost 1,000 feet high (305 metres) and are thus among the highest in England. Strong walkers are able to continue along the coastal path to Culbone and onwards to Porlock Weir and Porlock itself.

Motorists are sure of an interesting drive passing Countrygate

Lynmouth Harbour, many years before the disastrous flood destroyed so much of its fabric.

separating Devon and Somerset and then down Porlock Hill, one of the steepest roads in the country. The escape roads provided are the only comfort as car brakes become hotter and hotter as the long descent goes on. The first brave driver flogged his motor car up the hill as early as 1901. We are not sure whether we love Porlock because it is beautiful with its quaint streets, mixture of thatch and coloured stones or because of the relief of arriving once again at the foot of the hill in safety. There are, however, two slightly less terrifying ways into Porlock – both toll roads, one very narrow, the other wider and providing magnificent views over the sea.

Porlock is described in *Lorna Doone* and specific reference is made to the thatched Ship Inn which was one of the haunts of the highwayman Tom Faggus and the importance of Porlock market is also mentioned. John Ridd bought powder for his blunderbuss at 'The Spit and Gridiron' shop and returned to Dare by urging his horse up the frightening hill. At the turn of the 19th century the poet Robert Southey stayed at the Ship Inn and Coleridge, who was his brother-in-law, also knew the area. Situated on the

The thatched Anchor Inn, although somewhat restored, has retained its 14th-century characteristics.

main street is a small museum and information centre which is usually open during the summer season.

At present Porlock is a Jekyll and Hyde of a village with ugly structures mingling with attractive residences of stone and thatch with some colourful examples surrounding the mainly 13th-century church dedicated to St. Dubricus. He was one of the outstanding figures of the Celtic church in Wales during the 6th-century. Legend has it that Dubricus was the priest who married King Arthur to Guinevere. It is highly likely that there was a Saxon church on the present site and there was also a harbour with the sea lapping against its walls during the same period. Danish invaders landed here in AD 918 and set out to loot the area. The present church is probably 13th century in origin and there is on display a clock which has no hands and no face but merrily chimed the hours until the 1890s by striking its tenor bell. It was built by Roger the clockmaker from Barnstaple around 1400.

There are interesting effigies including one of a 13th-century knight, thought to be that of Sir Simon Fitz-Rogers, whose family owned the Manor of Porlock at the time of his death in 1306.

The real gem, however, is the tomb of John Harrington who is said to have fought at Agincourt in 1415, and who died three years later. This tomb is topped by an almost life-size alabaster effigy of the soldier and his wife. The spire of the church was

Culbone is said to be the smallest church in England.

blown down during a storm and there are two legends concerned with this event. One tells of a terrible storm in 1703 which blew the spire up over the cliff to fall on Culbone Church and added a spire to its little tower! The second suggests that masons were replacing the spire when the hunt passed by and the men followed the hounds and failed to come back. Whatever the real truth of the matter, the tower made of overlapping wooden tiles certainly looks unfinished.

Porlock itself is now a mile from the sea, but at Porlock Weir a small harbour was constructed to overcome silting and is surrounded by cottages with roofs of slate and thatch including the 14th-century Ship Inn which is thatched on the outside and equally traditional on the inside. We have spent many happy hours just sitting on the harbour wall watching the pleasure boats, whilst on other occasions we have made the two-mile walk to what is said to be the smallest church in England. Unfortunately there is no circular route and having seen the church the same path must be followed in reverse. This does not matter and in any case two miles downhill seems short after the climb through woodlands full of flowers, broad-leaved trees and evidence of the busy life of the charcoal burners who lived and worked in these woods for most of the year.

Culbone is a peaceful little church, its chancel 13ft 6ins by 10ft, its nave 21ft 6ins by 12ft 4ins and therefore having a total length of 35 feet. A notice in the church assures us that it will seat 38 people in great discomfort! Set in a delightful little dell a church probably existed here in the 7th century. Its ancient name was Kitnor deriving from the Anglo-Saxon 'cyta' meaning a cave and 'ore' meaning the shore, and here a church was built to celebrate the teaching of St Bueno (Kil Beun), a Welsh saint born in the late 6th century. The present building dates from the late 12th century although one window looks as if it may be Saxon and alterations were made in the 13th and 14th centuries with the spire added about 1810. Small bells were cast for this small church, one in the 17th century and the other in the 14th century and this is quite likely to be the oldest bell in West Somerset. The impressive churchyard cross was erected only in 1966 but on top of a 15th-century base.

Close to the church is a neat little hut in which light refreshments are available. You brew your own tea or coffee and place the money in an honesty box. This is walking country, as is the area described in Chapter 9 which takes us from Porlock to the Minehead area. Now, however, it is time to explore Lorna Doone country.

CHAPTER 8

Lorna Doone's Exmoor

Many people visit Exmoor having read R.D. Blackmore's novel *Lorna Doone* and proceed to seek out the places mentioned. Indeed, they use the book like a travel guide and obviously this can lead to criticism of the author. Clearly this is wrong, as the whole ethos of a novel is to allow a degree of poetic licence whilst using existing landmarks as a basis – we stress the word basis – for description. The object of this chapter, and other smaller sections of this book, is to provide a modern guide to Doone country. The present chapter will consider first the life of Blackmore himself, then the factual basis of the Doone legend and thirdly will consider the so-called 'Doone valley'.

Richard Doddridge Blackmore had a rather unfortunate early childhood. He was born on June 7th 1825 at Longworth in Berkshire, the third son of the Reverend John Blackmore, who had been educated at Exeter College, Oxford, which was, as its name implies, the seat of learning for the sons of Devonshire. Within weeks of Richard's birth his mother had died during an epidemic of typhus which also claimed his mother's twin sister and some family servants. His grief-stricken father had returned to his beloved Devonshire first to attend to the spiritual needs of the folk of Culmstock, from there moving to Ashford and then to Heanton Court which was the home of his late wife's family. Richard was not involved in these moves but was cared for by Miss Knight, his aunt, who was well-to-do and lived in a fine Tudor mansion close to Porthcawl. Miss Knight then continued the family tradition by marrying into the Church after which she moved to the village of Earlsfield in Oxfordshire, taking Richard with her to join her husband. Although he was well treated by his aunt at all times this unusual atmosphere in which he spent his early years may well account for his somewhat introverted character.

He returned to his father's house after John Blackmore had remarried a delightful lady and when the time came for his education to begin, he attended South Molton's grammar school which was established in the 16th century. He later moved to King's School at Bruton and then Blundell's school in Tiverton. Richard proved to be of scholarly disposition although somewhat liable to be bullied which may well have been the source of later inspiration for the first chapter of Lorna Doone when young John Ridd has to stand up to mindless aggression. Despite this Richard appears to have been happy at school and to have worked hard enough to merit a place at Exeter College in 1843 where the life of an Oxford student seems also to have suited him very well. More memories of R.D. Blackmore's childhood are depicted in other books especially *Cumstock* which was the model for his novel *Perlycross.*

University is one thing, a salary-earning career is another. Why R.D. Blackmore chose law instead of the clergy is not clear although he may well have hero-worshipped one of his ancestors who in 1604 had become a successful Solicitor General. This was Sir John Doddridge from whom Blackmore's middle name originated. In 1849 Richard was admitted to the Middle Temple but soon established a preference for accepting briefs from the Inner Temple and Chancery bars. He was called to the bar himself in 1852 and continued to practise until 1857 when his health became suspect and he was advised to seek alternative employment, preferably out of doors.

About this time he married Lucy Maguire, a Roman Catholic who became an Anglican out of respect for her husband; although the marriage seems to have been happy and lasted for 32 years until Lucy's death there were no children. Evidence suggests that Richard would have liked children and he accepted the responsibility of godfather to a number of infants and the artist Francis Armstrong named his daughter 'Lorna' in recognition of the book. It is said, upon what solid evidence we know not, that R.D. Blackmore was even asked to sponsor Noël Coward but declined because some of his godchildren had died of spinal meningitis and he was beginning to become superstitious. Whatever his feelings were he does seem to have aged gracefully and was long remembered after his death as a gentle soul.

After a short spell as a schoolmaster at Wellesley House School in Twickenham, Blackmore's health began once more to cause concern, but he had already begun to turn inwards to his writing and had published a number of rather undistinguished books of poetry of which *Poems by Melanter* received some praise if few royalties. In 1860 he bought 16 acres of land at Bushy Park near Hampton Court and built *Comer* House from which to base a horticultural business which gave him the essential fresh air his doctors were constantly recommending and the time to write which his own intellect demanded. Although it would seem that he had no horticultural training, Richard's childhood had been spent close to the soil and he had an interest in all things natural – indeed some of his best writings do rival the works of Hardy although the latter was obviously a much more skilful and consistent novelist. Blackmore did, however, have a number of eminent scientific friends including especially Professor Richard Owen. It is a pity that *Gomer* House was demolished in 1938 as it might have made an interesting museum dedicated to the life of R.D. Blackmore, but on reflection we feel that the Doone valley itself is perhaps the best memorial.

Although he had written *Clara Vaughan, Cradock Nowell, The Maid of Sker* and *Alice Lorraine* before *Lorna Doone* R.D. Blackmore is rather unfairly regarded as a one-book author. He began to research Lorna in the 1860s drawing heavily on his Exmoor family background, even though he himself was never a permanent resident within the area. His grandfather, however, was one time vicar of Oare and also of Combe Martin, whilst his uncle was the rector of the village of Charles near Lynton. The researches for *Lorna Doone* seem to have taken about seven years and involved stays at The Rising Sun hotel in Lynton, Withypool, Oare, Charles, the Ship Inn at Porlock and visits to a number of other villages and small towns which were woven into the text. The actual penning of the first draft has been precisely documented by the family as beginning in 1867 and the final full stop forged around six of the clock on the evening of 15th April 1868. The family were also adamant that the actual writing was done at Twickenham despite many Exmoor villages attracting visitors with the statement that 'Lorna Doone was written here'. We may, however, be splitting hairs as Blackmore must have eaten and stayed at several places during the period of research and some of these will be described later in this chapter and in other chapters of this book.

Initially the author had great difficulty in getting a publisher to accept *Lorna Doone*, despite the fact that Blackmore already had seven other books in print. Indeed several publishers considered the new work at length before rejecting it; eventually Sampson Low after some critical debate printed only 500 copies and even then sold only 300 of the print run. *Lorna Doone* was not a success and would have continued to gather dust if it had not been for a chance event; in 1870 Princess Louise, daughter of Queen Victoria, married a Scottish peer, the Marquis of Lorne. A reviewer whose history must have been somewhat shaky suggested that Blackmore's book was based on the ancestors of the Princess's new husband. Sampson Low reprinted again and again, *Lorna Doone* became a classic and R.D. Blackmore, who died on 20th January, 1900, joined the literary greats. Such is luck, although the author gained little financial reward. Perhaps he was happy with the fame, although he did comment that 'If I had dreamed that it would be more than a book of the moment, the descriptions of scenery – which I know as well as I know my own garden – would have been kept nearer to the fact'. Any tourist who insults Blackmore's precise descriptions should bear the author's own words in mind, but also be thankful that it was the popularity of *Lorna Doone* which led to the improvement of the road from Minehead and Porlock and for the increased popularity of Lynton and Lynmouth. Hotels and farmers who live from 'tourist money' should not forget the gentle soul of R.D. Blackmore in their prayers.

On the subject of facts, we must now go on to consider the legend of the Doones on which Blackmore based his novels. Such a law-despising family did indeed exist and there is no doubt *Lorna Doone* was based on the writings of the Reverend Matthew Mundy who lived at Lynton from 1833 and who became fascinated by the local folk memories of the Doones. Mundy discovered that one Mrs Ursula Johnson née Babb had been a fountain of knowledge regarding the Doones and although she died in 1826 many details had been passed on to a friend named Ursula Fry who died in 1856 at the age of 90. It is this lady who seems to have provided many of the details which Matthew Mundy committed to paper. Roger A. Burton in his excellent book, *The Heritage of Exmoor*, points out that in the 1841 census of Lynton, Ursula Fry is listed as a 75-year-old laundress. It may not be a coincidence that John Ridd's servant in *Lorna Doone* is named John Fry!

This postcard of around 1920 shows Lorna Doone Farm at Malmesmead.

It is said that the Doones were 17th-century Scottish aristocrats who had caused offence by their lawlessness and settled well away from the scenes of their initial crimes in an almost hidden valley on Exmoor where they lived in a time warp, a sort of cruel *Brigadoon.* Whatever the truth of the matter, the late 1850s saw the publication in eight instalments in *The Leisure Hours Magazine* of the tale of the Doones of Exmoor. The author described the Doones of Bagworthy as 'a gang of blood thirsty robbers who haunted the roads of Exmoor' in the days of the Stuart kings and here in a nutshell is the synopsis of Blackmore's novel. In 1901 Ida M. Browne wrote an article in the *West Somerset Press* in which she claimed, under the name of Audrie Doone, to be descended from the Scottish lord Sir Endsor Doone.

There is, they say, no smoke without fire, and no-one who has visited Doone country in winter with the snow driving across the grey valley would dare to argue. There is a strange, still and haunting feeling hereabouts even on glorious days of summer, a feeling which guarantees that the Doones' legend and the stream of visitors they attract will never dry up.

There is only one place to begin the exploration of Lorna Doone's Exmoor and that is the area around Oare Church which lies almost equidistant between Robber's Bridge and Malmesmead. Our first introduction was on foot with the autumn mist rolling down the valley and absorbing the aroma of wood smoke from the sturdy farmsteads overlooking Oare Water. At Robber's Bridge the Oare is joined by Weir Water, the two forming a rushing foaming boil of white water crushing between overhanging rocks and beneath a charming little packhorse bridge. Nearby is a substantial car park and picnic site. Following the river downstream leads past the pretty little hamlet of Oareford and then down to Oare Church set into the side of a hill. There has probably been a church here since Saxon times and in Domesday Oare Water is mentioned as an ancient British river. It had a chaplain in 1225 and there is documentary evidence that Robert of Oare killed Walter the chaplain and also injured his son. The account of the church on display in the present building comments that Oare was rather small to have warranted a chaplain, even in those days, but its influence over this wild area must have been profound.

The roof of the nave and the inner chancel are described as the Waggon type, which was a simple construction much favoured by early architects which meant that all they had to do was to follow the shape of a waggon, invert it and stand it on solid walls. In most early churches the ceiling would have been painted but no trace remains of this at Oare. There are typical examples of 18th-century furniture including box pews with doors and a pulpit reading desk. At the time that Blackmore set Lorna Doone – around 1680 – these would not have been present, but there would have been plain wooden benches such as those seen at Culbone Church near Porlock Weir. The nave of Oare Church is also typically Georgian but the east window is modern and so is the chancel to the east of the screen. It is the font which gives a clue to the age of the church with scholars dating the basin from the 12th century although the stem and the base are probably 19th century. Of special interest is the piscina which is in the form of a well-preserved head, probably a carving of St Ducumen. This obviously is pre-Reformation in origin since this was one of the catholic features which was not required in the more austere protestant service. A piscina was a carved stone bowl set into the wall of the church and in which the chalices used in the mass could be washed. There was usually a drain hole leading to the exterior of the church.

There are three bells in the solid square tower which were cast as late as 1873, but an earlier bell dated 1770 has been retained and is now an integral and pleasant sounding part of the chiming clock. A sensitive restoration was carried out in the spring of 1991.

Near to the door is a copy of a plaque commemorating Blackmore, the original being kept in Exeter Cathedral. He chose Oare Church in which to set the wedding of John Ridd and Lorna Doone because he knew it so well. His grandfather, John Blackmore, had been rector of Oare from 1809 to 1842, although he does not seem to have ministered to his flock very often, leaving the day-to-day running of the church to a poorly paid and probably not very well qualified curate.

Blackmore describes Carver Doone shooting down Lorna as she was being married and the evil man aims his gun through a single window in the old chancel to the left of the screen. Some with a good knowledge of both the church and the capabilities of 17th-century weapons have pointed out that at this range Lorna would have been blown to pieces and suggest that the gun could only have been discharged at the west end of the church. This again underlies the refusal of some commentators to allow the author any trace of poetic licence. Apart from using the church, Blackmore also seems to have made use of the parish registers with the Ridd family always prominent, a trend which still continues. A John Ridd was churchwarden at Oare from 1914 to 1925 and his grandson was holding the same office in the 1980s.

Malmesmead is another charming little hamlet, straddling the Devon-Somerset border and which inspired Blackmore. The village is bisected by a stream. Here is the ancient ford, now overlooked by a quaint bridge which is so narrow that large vehicles still use the ford. Across the ford is Lorna Doone farm, now a rather up-market shop, but it is easy to see why it inspired Blackmore. This is walkers' country and close to the bridge is a spacious car park overlooking Badgworthy Water, which Blackmore described as flowing out of the Doone Valley. From Malmesmead it flows on to meet Oare Water where they merge to become the East Lyn. On the opposite side of the bridge to the car park is the head-quarters of Exmoor Natural History Society. The centre is open to visitors from mid-May to September each

Wednesday and Thursday from 1.30 pm to 5 pm and admission is free. Between late July and early September the centre also opens on Tuesdays. There is a self-operated audiovisual display covering the geology, history and natural history of the area and there is also a book stall with a good selection of maps. Children are made particularly welcome and are sure to enjoy the electrically operated games which help in the identification of the local wildlife. On Wednesdays from mid-June to mid-September a free guided walk, which is described as 'gentle', leaves the centre to explore Doone country and there is also an excellent little picnic site. There is a limited amount of bed and breakfast accommodation available at local farms and also one or two well-appointed places to camp.

For those who wish to walk on their own, the car park forms an ideal base for several bracing strolls. There are two good routes into the Doone Valley, which has also remained surprisingly free from the excesses of commercialism. A riverside path can be followed on payment of a nominal sum to the local farmer who usually leaves a leather pouch hanging over a gate into which honest folk drop their coins. A higher path above the valley can be followed free of charge, but we prefer to enjoy both routes with a break for lunch between. Our introduction to this area was on a December day of biting cold with sleet in the air, during which we watched a herd of almost 20 red deer composed of hinds and their calves and just beyond these we could see through our binoculars a small group of Exmoor ponies seeking the shelter of a stout stand of hawthorns, the branches of which were still heavy with soft red fruit. As the animals brushed beneath the laden branches they disturbed a mixed flock of redwing, fieldfare and blackbird which were greedily feeding. We returned on a breezy April morning with only the sound of a soaring skylark for company and again on a day of blazing June sunshine when we watched energetic children fishing for bullhead and gudgeon. We were reminded once more of Blackmore's novel, when John Ridd ventured into the Doone Valley to catch gudgeon for his sick mother. He fell into Badgworthy Water and almost drowned, his near escape being witnessed by the young Lorna – the first meeting of children eventually destined to become happy lovers. And then there was the day we watched a buzzard soaring high on the thermals of air rising from the rocks heated by the strengthening early morning August sun. Despite being at the height of the holiday season we were alone. This is God's own quiet country. And John Ridd's. And Lorna's!

Beyond Malmesmead is the larger village of Brendon which is situated just to the north-west of the Doone Valley and enclosed between steep moors and the East Lyn River which swirls on its way towards Lynmouth. Blackmore knew it well and may well have used a guest house called Brendon Forge as a basis for the scene in which John Ridd described the muscular smith stepping outside to cool the red hot irons in the cool waters of the river. At this time John was on his way to what Blackmore called Ley Manor which was probably based upon Lee Abbey beyond Lynton and which is described in chapter 7.

Some villages including Malmesmead can be visited at any time whilst others should be savoured on a special occasion. Brendon, which means the hill of the brambles, is such a place and on the third Saturday in October it is seen at its vibrant best. This is the date of the pony fair which has been a feature of the district for around two centuries. The Exmoor ponies are all actually owned and branded by local farmers who once herded them over the moor to Cheriton but the sale is now held at Leeford farm in the village, and takes place on the following Monday. Any unsold animals were once herded to Bampton, but are now transported in horse boxes ready for the sale which takes place there at the end of the month.

Badgworthy Water lay within the parish of Brendon and was not subject to the influence of Oare; Badgworthy itself was a medieval hamlet which once belonged to the Pomeroy family who donated land to the knights of the Hospital of Jerusalem. By 1430, however, their buildings had fallen into a sad state of neglect but over the centuries, poor squatters may have attempted to farm the land. No doubt Blackmore visited the pile of stones and his imagination breathed life into them to produce the settlement of the Doones!

Thus Badgworthy has a religious settlement long since deserted but the story of its present parish church is just as fascinating; it is situated just over a mile from the village and 700 feet (213 metres) above sea level. It is dedicated to St Brendon, a Celtic missionary, although the ground on which the church stands was not the site of a Saxon building. Why is this so? Actually the

The Simonsbath Hotel is one of the most historic houses to be found in Exmoor.

church was moved stone by stone from Cheriton in 1738 although a rather incongruous tower was added in 1838. The font, however, is ancient and its three bells were forged around 1500.

In an area famous for quaint inns and tangles of cottages, Rockford still stands out in its beauty with the Staghunter's Inn overlooked to the south by Brendon Common, the Chains and the Exe plain. Here is the catchment area for the rivers of Exmoor and no-one who has walked these heights in a snow storm or in heavy rain can doubt its efficiency in this regard. We were once caught here in a hail storm which struck on a January evening totally without warning. The streams seemed to rise as if someone had turned on a tap and lightning flashed and thunder cracked like gunfire. On the coastal cliffs at Lynton a flock of sheep was struck by lightning and killed. Within five minutes we were both soaked to the skin and felt in real need of a flask of coffee and energy-giving chocolate by the time we reached our car. The hail had started when we were less than half a mile from the car park. Such is the fury of Exmoor – true weather for the Doones.

Before leaving the Doone country, three other nearby settlements should also be explored, namely Simonsbath, Exford and Withypool. Simonsbath is a small yet historic village in the valley of the River Barle. From remote times the hamlet, as it still remains despite a new but small housing estate, had a strategic importance since it was sited at the junction of several moorland tracks. This no doubt explains why James Boevey, the first commoner to obtain the freehold of what had been the Royal Forest of Exmoor, set up his base at Simonsbath in 1652. He constructed an impressive house for himself, now the Simonsbath House Hotel and above the old kitchen fireplace the date 1654 is carved into the oak beam.

Throughout the period when Cromwell's parliament ruled Britain, much royal land was sold off to commoners, but following his restoration in 1660 Charles II reclaimed his heritage. In many cases he was not as unfeeling as one might imagine and Boevey was allowed to remain as a tenant until his death. After this his house was used as a base by the wardens of the forest. Boevey is still commemorated in the name of an attractive restaurant adjacent to the Simonsbath House Hotel. In 1819, however, the forest – or at least 10,000 acres (4,000 hectares) was once more purchased by a commoner. John Knight was a successful ironmaster from Worcestershire with great pretentions to be a gentleman and he paid £50,000 to establish himself among the land-owning classes with the intention of founding a dynasty. Although not always popular with the locals 'The Knights of Exmoor' does have a certain ring to it. He had the ambition to build an even finer house at Simonsbath after establishing his base there in 1827, but for some reason he failed to follow the project through and the incomplete shell was finally demolished in 1900.

It was John's first son Frederick Knight, however, who had a more permanent effect upon the area. He loved the moor, but wished to tame it and established the family as efficient sheep and horse breeders. Less successful was the effort to follow the example set in the Wild West of America by driving a herd of Highland cattle down from Scotland. Harnessing the waters of Pinkworthy Pond was another of the Knight's projects which almost succeeded. He did, however, build new and improve old farms for his tenants, make dramatic improvements to the roads which, until then had often been mere tracks, and laid out miles of beech hedges to shelter the livestock from the fierce Exmoor winters. These hedges add a delightful russet colour to the winter scene as beech holds its leaves much longer than most deciduous trees, whilst the spring green of the new foliage is also a delight to the walker and essential for the survival of the farm animals. The wild deer are not slow to seek the shelter of Knight's hedges when the icy winds sweep across the otherwise open moor.

What would have happened if Frederick's son had not died in 1879 at the age of only 28 it is difficult to imagine, but we must assume that the father's sudden loss of interest and ambition was detrimental to the moor. St Luke's Church, built in 1856 on a hill overlooking Simonsbath, looks a distinguished building and appears much older than it actually is, but is a testimony to the Knights of Exmoor, a dynasty sadly cut off in its adolescence.

Down in the hamlet itself is a very attractive craft shop and working pottery plus the Exmoor Forest Hotel which often plays host to the exciting, colourful but controversial stag hunt. The real focus of the horse and hounds, however, is at Exford. Exford lies in the shelter of the River Exe Valley. A fine old bridge spans the river overlooked by the White Horse Inn which looks old and attractive enough to be the setting for a musical even though this honour is a part of alpine history.

Exford, however, has a music all of its own. On every day of the year the sound of horses' hooves echoes through the main street, whilst on some days the baying of the staghounds, whose kennels are close by, can set the blood stirring. As naturalists we can well understand the objections to such a hunt, but we would not wish the sound of the gathering of the hounds to disappear from the countryscene. Neither can we understand the cruelty of those who object to the hunt who seem to think it is acceptable to injure hound and horse to protect the deer. Such are their numbers on Exmoor that the population of red deer needs to be controlled. Perhaps humane shooting is the answer, but we doubt if the hunters would find chasing a trail of aniseed rather than live quarry an acceptable substitute.

Exford's parish church of St Mary Magdelene is set high on a hill overlooking the Exe Valley, and there is a view across to the crest of a hill along which runs a prehistoric track linking Bridgewater with Barnstaple. In those far off times the valleys were often flooded, always damp and a breeding ground for disease including malaria which was not finally eradicated from Britain until the 19th century. Sir Ronald Ross discovered that the blood-sucking female mosquito transmitted the malarial parasite from one human victim to another. Until the boggy land was cleared and drained and the mosquitoes sprayed the only quick, safe and healthy trade routes were literally the ancient high roads.

The present church of Exford dates from the middle of the 15th century although there have been a number of substantial alterations since this time. The oldest sections are the south aisle and the solid-looking west tower which suggests strength rather than architectural elegance. In the 19th century both the nave and the chancel were almost entirely rebuilt, but some atmosphere of the old church remains because of the arcade of pillars at the south aisle. A somewhat false feeling of antiquity is provided by the pre-Reformation rood screen which is much restored and is not in fact contemporary. It came from St Audries Church at West Quantoxhead beyond Minehead which was demolished in 1858. The screen was extensively restored in London before its installation at Exford in 1929. The choir stalls are also imports, this time from Queens College, Cambridge.

There was in all probability a Christian focus at Exford prior to the Norman Conquest and this is proved by the presence of the broken shaft of an Anglican cross probably used as a preaching point before a church was established. Originally the church was dedicated to the Celtic St Salvyn.

Many writers have pointed out that Exford should be regarded as the centre of Exmoor but it is too small, and we would say too unspoiled to be the focus for vast numbers of visitors and the honour is best left to the more substantial settlement of Dulverton described in Chapter 2. Exford is actually set around a substantial triangular screen which was purchased by the village community in 1906. It was once called 'The Fair Meadow' and sheep auctions were once held on it. Exford was used by Blackmore with Court Farm being associated with the highwayman Tom Faggus who played an heroic role in the life of John Ridd's sister. Once again the author seems to have based his names upon actual characters since one Thomas Fugars once lived at Court Farm, parts of which date from the 16th century. The house also had connections with the early establishment of the Methodist religion around Exford. Near the green is a private house which was once an unusual Methodist chapel containing two stained glass windows made by Sir Edmund Burne Jones in 1890. They were fashioned in the workshops of William Morris, an Oxford friend of Sir Edmund's. Originally they were part of Marylebone Chapel in London but were presented to Exford by the composer Cyril Scott, who lived at Exford during the Second World War, in memory of two of his friends – Holland Scott, a Durham professor who died at Lynmouth and Bertram Binyon, a singer and brother of the poet Lawrence Binyon who is buried at Dulverton.

Exford seems to have inspired many writers in addition to Blackmore including a trio of famous naturalists – Richard Jefferies, Henry Williamson and W.H. Hudson. Whilst gathering material for his book *Red Deer*, published in 1883, Jefferies walked the moor with Fred Heal, one of Exford's finest huntsmen. Henry Williamson famous, as already mentioned, for his *Tarka the Otter* spent many hours around the stables and kennels at Exford whilst writing *Life in a Devon Village*. We know how closely he examined the hounds to be able to describe the 'baleful yellow fire' which filled their eyes. W.H. Hudson was born in Argentina and learned to love its natural history before coming to England and writing some of the best prose ever written in praise of our more gentle and exploited countryside. He loved Exmoor and this is reflected in his description of the Exe which he likened to a 'silver serpent' that 'runs singing aloud'. We feel that Hudson, of all the writers tramping Exmoor, was the one to capture the wild spirit of the rivers.

Like Simonsbath, Exford developed largely because of the influence of the Knight family but it is proved beyond doubt that there was a ford over the Exe from the Bronze Age. A vital trade route, known as the Harepath, linked the Midlands with Cornwall and in medieval times a wooden bridge spanned the stream. This was later replaced by a stone structure, the latest only dating from around 1930. The first inn to serve the village was constructed around 1600, but it was only a rather primitive ale house. With the increase in trade and prosperity during the 19th century the landlord first extended the White Horse and then built the Crown in 1820. Both had, and still have, good stabling.

The Devon and Somerset Staghounds have been based here since 1875 and there are 65 couples of hounds and 30 horses cared for in the village. At the Old Hunt Forge the single remaining blacksmith is kept busy and always has a cheery wave for locals and visitors alike. Sensible spectators are also welcome at the meets which hunt regularly between August and late April. These dates are advertised in the *West Somerset Free Press.* Summer events including puppy shows are also held and are well advertised.

Before leaving Doone country a visit must be made to Withypool where Blackmore is said to have stayed whilst writing his masterpiece, although he probably only used The Royal Oak as a research base before returning to Teddington, which was then a village outside London, to write in earnest. Blackmore became friendly with the landlady, Mrs Tudball and sent her strawberry plants from his nursery and she in return made him some shirts. Near Withypool Bridge is a substantial car park from which run footpaths along the banks of the River Barle, one of the best leading to Tarr Steps (see Chapter 2). The Withypool area has been settled since prehistoric times and there are the remnants of a stone circle on Withypool Hill, and the Green Barrow and Brightworthy Barrows on Withypool Common. The latter has itself an interesting history as the law of common land takes us back to medieval England, when some farmers were allowed the freedom to graze cattle and sheep, cut turf and gather firewood within the forest. These commoners had duties to perform in exchange including herding the warden's livestock, perambulating the boundaries once every seven years and serving on the coroner's jury when anyone was found dead in the forest. When the forest was finally enclosed in 1818 and the Royal Rule became a thing of the past the Free Suitors, as the Commoners were called, were each allowed 31 acres of Withypool Common and in 1949 The Withypool Commoners' Association was formed and protects these ancient rights to the present day.

Although Withypool is the last of the villages with Doone connections to be described in this chapter, Blackmore used many other settlements in his book and most of these have been described in other chapters. We conclude this chapter with a brief summary of the plot of the novel with a happy ending – *Lorna Doone.*

The book is set in the always dangerous period covering the reigns of Charles II and James II between 1660 and the late 1680s. At this time the unsuccessful Monmouth Rebellion took place and this forms an integral part of the plot as does the activity of the terrible judge Jeffreys who also appears in Blackmore's tale.

The story begins at Blundell's school in Tiverton with John

being called home to be told that his father has been murdered by the Doones. The boy's love for his mother leads him to go in search of fish which she enjoyed and in his eagerness to be successful John is swept away in the current and is almost drowned. When he awakens the 14-year-old gets his first sight of Lorna Doone who helps him to avoid discovery by the evil band showing him a secret entrance to their domain. Although the memory of Lorna is with him from then on, seven years elapse before he once more plucks up courage to visit Doone country. This leads to the first of many increasingly affectionate meetings. Carver Doone has lecherous eyes on Lorna, but she is protected by Sir Ensor Doone until his death leaves her without a friend and in danger of being forced into a marriage.

John Ridd comes to Lorna's rescue and, in the midst of an horrendous snowstorm, carries her off to his family at Plover's Barrow Farm. The Doones did not take kindly to this and plot her return but other events also unfold revealing that Lorna was kidnapped as a child. She was not a descendant of Sir Ensor Doone but of even higher birth and related to the Scottish Dugals. Her mother's distant ancestors did include a Doone but had a close connection with the lords of Lorne. Marriage of such a high lady to an Exmoor farmer would have been difficult but all is possible in a fictional plot. Jan Ridd's assistance given to Lady Lorna's kinsman Earl Brandir of Lochawe enables James II to pardon him for his albeit innocent involvement in the Monmouth Rebellion and to bestow upon him a knighthood. The rebellion took place in 1685 when James, Duke of Monmouth, returned from exile to attempt the overthrow of James II who was a rather bigoted Catholic. During the journey from Lyme Regis to the battlefield at Sedgemoor close to Bridgewater some 6,000 West Countrymen rallied to his cause. Following their humiliating defeat many were tried and executed often pleading in vain for mercy at the hands of the infamous Judge Jeffreys.

The Judge, however, not without some advantage to himself, frees Lorna from a Chancery wardship and thus allows her to return with Sir John Ridd and marry him in Oare Church. Before the ceremony the law-abiding citizens of Exmoor decide they have had enough of the Doones and only the wily Carver manages to escape. Seconds after John and Lorna have exchanged their vows Carver sneaks to the church and shoots the bride.

Thinking her dead John sets off in grim pursuit, corners the last of the Doones at the Wizards Slough. After a fearsome struggle the wounded hero forces Carver into a bog and he disappears for ever into the slime.

Both John and Lorna recover from their ordeal and live a long and happy life together. The Doone valley should therefore be remembered as a place of happy birdsong and not as a dismal fog-bound area of gloom.

CHAPTER 9

Porlock to Minehead and Dunster

The modern road runs directly from Porlock to Minehead and now bypasses a number of small villages, each with a charm and beauty of its own. These are quiet spots in contrast to the seaside resort of Minehead and the medieval village of Dunster which are hives of activity at all times of the year and provide varied accommodation from which to explore Exmoor and the Brendon Hills.

We defy anyone turning off the A39 into Allerford not to gasp and remark that the village has been left totally untouched and unspoiled by time. Peace enfolds the little hump-backed bridge, to the right of which is the well-named Pack Horse guest house and across the ford is a red brick, thatched cottage with an external bread oven and with a porch supported by wooden pillars. Seen in summer with the morning sun reflected from it the cottage is lovely enough to bring a tear to the eye and many a naturalist standing on the bridge has been lucky enough to see nature's own colourful wonder – the kingfisher. We have not been so lucky but we have seen grey wagtail, dipper and a water vole, all indicators of the purity of the water. Before the bridge was built in the Middle Ages there was a ford here overlooked by 'aller' trees which was Saxon for the alder, which thrives by water. A steep climb from the bridge cottage leads to the National Trust-owned woodlands which clothe a graceful hill overlooking the village and from which footpaths lead to Selworthy. On almost all of the many occasions we have visited Allerford we have seen buzzards hovering over the woodland which is also home to all three species of woodpecker native to Britain – the green, great and lesser spotted woodpecker, the latter being by far the most rare. Also common in Allerford woods is the attractive treecreeper which moves up tree trunks like a clockwork mouse, its delicately curved bill prising insects from behind the loose bark.

Everything about Allerford is friendly and refined and even the surprisingly large car park is almost hidden. It is almost opposite the Rural Life Museum which is open from the end of

March to mid-October. It should, however, never be missed especially by families with children. It is housed in the old school house which was once used by the children of Allerford and Selworthy and a reminder of those far-off days can be seen on the wall where the bell still hangs. Inside there is a Victorian schoolroom with an assortment of clothes which visitors are allowed to wear. This is by far the best way to learn history, but there is also a fine collection of old photographs and craft demonstrations are regularly held. Outside is a croquet lawn and a picnic site. There are many larger museums than this one, but we know of none with a better feeling and it is well worth the very modest entry fee.

Before continuing along the A39 towards Minehead and looking for the turn-off left to Selworthy a short diversion should be made to Pylle's or Pile's Mill, once an integral part of the village until the A39 sliced through it. The mill is driven by water diverted from the River Aller along a leet leading to the overshot wheel. This means that the water is directed onto the top of the wheel which then 'falls' because of the weight of water. Allerford Mill was mentioned in Domesday and is thus of ancient origin. It is owned by the National Trust and open to the public. Because there is limited parking it is best to walk to Pile's Mill from Allerford.

Selworthy, approached along a narrow lane lined with holly and beech, is a picture postcard village dominated by the startling white church of All Saints which to us appears more Mediterranean than English. It is our favourite in the whole of Exmoor. This is the only local church which is still coated with a mixture of lime and tallow which provides good protection against the weather. Photographs taken in the 1880s show that many of the local churches were similarly coated.

The tower of All Saints is probably late 14th- or early 15th-century and is described as Early Perpendicular in style but the windows of the south aisle and the outer archway of the porch are perhaps a century later. The tower contains a clock, parts of which are said to be 400-years-old, and it still keeps good time and strikes the hour on the tenor bell, but strangely there is no exterior clock face. In 1875 during restoration work a number of frescoes were discovered on the walls. It was a pity that they were not discovered recently as the techniques required to restore

The brown hare is also hunted around Exmoor. What a delightful animal it is, equally at home on moorland and in the woods.

such wall paintings are now well known. The seating in the nave and in the aisles dates mainly from the 16th century; they were skilfully repaired in 1875, but unfortunately some box pews were removed at the same time.

The remains of a holy water stoop is seen in the porch and there is also a Norman font. The porch has an upper storey which is now used as a vestry; it opens towards the church and was once a balcony pew for the unfortunate Acland family from nearby Holnicote. The Aclands came to the area in the mid-18th century and their various mishaps were faithfully recorded by their own historian Anne Acland. In 1745 Sir Thomas Acland, the 7th Baron, married Elizabeth Dyke and thus acquired three substantial estates in Somerset. These were Pixton near Dulverton, Tetton near Taunton and Holnicote. The new owner was a sporting man, as were many of the aristocracy of the time and for 30 years he was master of the North Devon Staghounds. Then fate took a hand. Holnicote burned down in 1779; Sir Thomas died in 1785; John his eldest son died after being held captive during the American War of Independence; his grandson, another John, died at the age of seven; the tragedies continued with the death of his youngest son in 1794.

Then came a period of glorious recovery with the 10th Baronet Thomas Acland (1787-1871) leading the way and transforming Selworthy parish. Between 1810 and 1826 he caused 80,000 trees to be planted and improved his estate beyond measure, a task now continued by the National Trust. When he was only 21 Thomas married the daughter of the banker Henry Hoare, who revealed his business feelings when told that Lydia and her husband were temporarily short of funds and would be obliged to live for a while on their wits. He commented that two people more unfitted to live by their wits he had never known.

They did, however, survive and although Holnicote was not their main residence they loved it and even rebuilt it following a second disastrous fire in 1851.

Those who stand at the church and then follow the signposted footpaths to North Hill, Bury Castle, Selworthy Beacon and Allerford have cause to thank the Aclands and the National Trust who followed them. Many walk the woods and are provided with spacious car parks close to the church. In 1887 the naturalist writer Richard Jefferies, by that time mortally ill, walked the Selworthy area and wrote delightfully of red squirrels playing in the grounds of Holnicote House and humble bees pollinating the holly flowers which would thus produce berries for Christmas. We had both read Jefferies before we ever set foot in Selworthy Woods with its tumbling streams of white water, swathes of colourful flowers and cascades of bird song. Jefferies had prepared us and we were not disappointed.

Those walking from Selworthy Church up through the glorious woodlands following the signs to Bury Castle often express disappointment that they have failed to find the stately pile. There are extensive earthworks on the top of the steep hill and in Saxon times the summit may well have been surmounted by a stout wooden palisade. Not a stone keep and drawbridge to be sure but pretty fearsome nevertheless and a strong deterrent to the invading Danes. Bury Castle was probably so defended from Neolithic times. Selworthy Beacon would provide an early warning system with its blazing bonfire easily seen from the centre of Exmoor and from Minehead. It was part of a communication chain operating throughout the West Country.

If the castle and the beacon spell war and conflict, then Selworthy Green, below the church, spells fairytale and fantasy and shows the Aclands' care and enjoyment for their estate. Owned by the National Trust since 1944, there is now an information centre and shop and the green looks fit to grace any chocolate box, with a tangle of thatched cottages including Periwinkle Cottage which serves excellent teas in the season. If Beatrix Potter, who actually knew the area, had not written in the Lake District then she could surely have found inspiration in this delightful spot. In 1810 Sir Thomas Acland converted a dilapidated farm and its outbuildings to produce enchanting dwellings for his servants to live in. The black and white thatchings remain today providing a lasting reminder of an often absentee landlord but with no absence of taste.

Almost opposite the green is the 15th-century tithe barn, not open to the public but it is the exterior which is of interest anyway and it is still possible to find, despite the erosion caused by centuries of Exmoor weather, carvings of a pig, lambs and a wheatsheaf. Here the local farmers would have brought their taxes paid in kind to the church and which kept their priest in food.

Those with cars should, on return to the parking area near the church, make two further short pilgrimages to Lynch Chapel-of-Ease and St Leonard's Chapel-of-Ease at Tivington. Both are in regular use and were restored in the 1990s thanks to the heroic efforts of the small local community and donations from the summer visitors who cannot resist the lure of the white church on the hill.

Tivington is located around half a mile off the A39 along the road to Wootton Courtenay. The chapel was constructed around 1350 for the Cluniac priory of Montacute near Yeovil by the landowner Sir Ralph de Middelney but following the dissolution of the monasteries in the 1530s the chapel was no longer used as a place of worship. After use as a store house for a cottage built against the east window and blocking it up, it then became a barn and in the 19th century was used as a dame school. The latter function meant that after a gap of around 300 years St Leonard's was once more serving the community. In 1896 it was finally brought back into religious service and further restorations were tastefully carried out in 1940 and in 1990. Two features are of special interest, namely the open fireplace and in particular the roof; it is the only church building in the Diocese of Bath and Wells still to have the typical West Country thatch composed of wheaten reed.

Anyone for whom thatch conjures up a desire to discover traditional Exmoor and who enjoys walking should continue on a short distance to Wooton Courtenay which is constructed of pink stone over which tumble a profusion of summer flowers. It looks to be what the name 'Wooton' suggests – a place in the woods which in the 12th century was governed by the Courteney family, the earls of Devon.

This is walking, riding and hunting country. The kennels of the Minehead Harriers are here; it is not only the deer which are hunted over Exmoor. Foxes are also chased and the harriers are especially trained to hunt the brown hare. For those of quieter disposition there are walks from the village which lies below Grabbist Hill, over unspoiled countryside to Dunkery, Dunster, Tivington, Robin How and the Horner Valley. The area is a naturalist's paradise, but there is plenty to see in the village itself including a water-powered pottery and yet another attractive church. The problem, however, is to find it, as from the narrow street it is concealed behind a screen of high yew trees. The tower would look more fitting as part of a pigeon loft but is officially described as a saddleback tower and converted to its present shape during restorations in 1866 which involved rebuilding the chancel and the addition of an attractive south porch.

The interior of the church always seems to have a lightness which is made even more refreshing in the warmer months of the year when it never seems to be without flowers. Of particular note are the carved waggon roofs depicting eagles to represent St John, a pelican to symbolise piety, whilst the bosses show St George and the dragon – the victory of good over evil. There is also a rather unusual arrangement in two of the solid pillars in the form of niches which before the Reformation housed small statues of St Lawrence and St Christopher.

To find Selworthy's second little chapel it is necessary to turn back along the A39 to Allerford and then follow the signs to yet another village of breathtaking beauty at Bossington. Lynch Chapel is about halfway between the two villages sandwiched between a tiny packhorse bridge and a farm. The latter is open

Lynch Chapel is a delightful little building, governed from Selworthy.

from 10.30 am to 4.30 pm from 6th April to the end of September and provides a children's play area, a picnic site plus a display of young ducks, hens and geese in a farmyard surrounded by thatched buildings. We once heard a child compare this scene with Camberwick Green and we had to admit that all that was missing was the happy music.

The chapel itself is always open and although the precise date of its construction is not known it probably dates from around 1520. Although the stained glass in the east window is modern, it is important as it tells the history of the chapel, and especially of the parish of Bossington. This formed part of the possessions of Athelney from AD 900 until the dissolution of the monasteries in the late 1530s. The abbey was founded by Alfred the Great to celebrate his victory over the Danes at Eddington in 878 AD. Hence we find the seal of the abbey and the arms of Alfred set out in the window. The remaining coats of arms are those of the most important landowners governing Bossington. The de Talbots held it from 1145 to 1316 when it passed to John Wytton who retained the arms and thus only the de Talbots are depicted. In 1425 Henry Sydenham came into possession of the manor by marriage, and his descendants remained in control until it was purchased by William Blackford in 1694. After only two generations the estate again changed hands by the marriage of an heiress who became Elizabeth Dyke. In 1744 the same thing happened and Sir Thomas Acland added Bossington to his expanding estate. The coat of arms beneath the mitre is that of the Diocese of Bath and Wells who are the present administrators.

Those who get the chance should not fail to attend the occasional services which are held in this chapel and also at Tivington.

Like Selworthy, much of Bossington is owned by the National Trust and in the warmer months splendid cream teas are usually on offer among the cluster of thatched cottages. There is a quiet car park overlooked by the tree-covered towering bulk of Bossington Hill which is part of North Hill. From the information board a network of footpaths radiate out down to the pebbled beach, out onto Hurlstone Point and through trees to Allerford. This is also a naturalists' country and W.H. Hudson's writings of fox and badger, otter and deer, buzzard and barn owl made his *Wild Exmoor through the Year* a classic. Hudson, however, was but a visitor and Bossington had its own resident countryman. E.W. Hendy described redstart, dipper, curlew, yellowhammer and greenfinch all of which can be seen today, but he also mentions the corncrake. This is sadly no longer part of the British countryside with the exception of some of the Hebridean islands which have retained the old agricultural methods. In the days before artificial fertilisers, crops grew more slowly and the corncrake could raise its young and have them flying before the crop was harvested. Those birds which nested late would be ignored by the farmer who harvested by hand. Once mechanised harvesting developed, the breeding birds were literally mowed down. Thus the corncrakes of Exmoor have long gone, but many of the other aspects of a more gentle age have survived.

Long before we met, we had both visited Minehead on holiday in the summer; our first visit together was altogether less memorable as a driving wind whipped up white horses on a grey sea and despite the shelter of the North Hill both we and our black labrador were in danger of being blown off our feet. On the beach we met a wind-tanned resident, with his flowing white beard streaming in the wind, who was carrying a metal detector. He laughed and told us that Minehead weather was always mild and any deterioration was due to Mother Leakey. This lady seems to have been easy going until her death in 1634 when her favourite necklace was given away to someone she did not like. Her son, who was a fisherman, bore the brunt of Mother Leakey's anger and she whistled up a storm each time his boat headed for harbour. Not content with just 'whistling in the wind' she also appeared in ghostly form and in his novel *Rokeby* Sir Walter Scott mentions the whistling ghost of Minehead.

Whilst many seaside resorts have a history dating from the mid-19th century, Minehead and the district which surrounds it are steeped in ancient history. Most historians accept that the name derives from the Old English 'Myned' meaning a hill. Half a day spent climbing up through the town to the summit and the remaining ancient farms called West and East Myne is well worth the effort. Looking out from the top of the hill shows clearly that the coastline has altered over the centuries. What is now Minehead Bay was once an area of woodland, and fossilised wood from these trees is washed up on the sandy beach at the time of a Mother Leakey storm. At one time the sea lapped Dunster and its castle is easily seen from Minehead, especially from North Hill.

The summit of the hill was perhaps once crowned by a hill fort similar to Bury Castle described in the last chapter and there is another above Dunster called Bats Castle. On May Day each year, Minehead remembers its ancient past in the form of its Hobby Horse Festival which compares more than favourably with that at Padstow. The streets echo to music and laughter, colourful costumes and flowers are everywhere and given the weather everyone is out of doors joining in the fun. Historians, or perhaps it would be better to say 'folklorists' disagree about the origins of the hobby horse, but we would prefer to accept the view that it is a pagan ceremony to welcome in the spring and say a happy farewell to the long dark days of winter. There are some who say that the ceremony is Minehead's reversal of the Trojan horse story, when in the 9th century the inhabitants frightened the Danes with huge wooden horses, although it seems to us that only cold steel would affect the intrepid invaders from the sea. Whatever its origins, May Day in Minehead is an event to be savoured.

The walk up from sea level to St Michael's Church provides the essence of old Minehead. There are many reasons to stop and rest on the flight of tiled and cobbled steps which pass a delightful blend of red and yellow cottages, some thatched and many with tall chimneys. The church itself should be explored slowly, most of it dating from the 14th and 15th centuries. Inside there is an illuminated missal dated around 1400, a 15th-century font, a carved screen of around 1500, a 17th-century pulpit and even the modern age has contributed its own elegance in the form of a brass lantern and some fine wrought ironwork.

The view from the church down towards the harbour is spectacular and it was here that the prosperity of the town was focused before the age of the tourist. In 1616 the Luttrel family of Dunster Castle provided the town with a stone harbour to replace a flimsy wooden structure which had suffered grievous damage from the storms. This has certainly stood the test of time, although the harbour was strengthened in 1682 and was substantially enlarged in 1901. In the 17th and 18th centuries considerable trade was carried on with Ireland, the West Indies and with the Southern States of America especially Virginia prior to the Wars of Independence. Trade was also carried on with France, Spain and the Mediterranean which together bought 4,000 barrels of herring a year from Minehead alone until the shoals moved away from this area of coast. Minehead Harbour handled wine from France and Spain and exported wool, linen, coal, hides and even live animals bred on Exmoor. Salt was also a valuable commodity, and what is now the tiny St Peter's Chapel was once a salt store. Another reminder of the past life of the harbour is a splendid row of fishermens' cottages. The fishermen had more than a religious attachment to their church for in stormy weather a lantern was kept burning in the tower.

A master mariner named Robert Quirke had cause to bless the light and in the midst of a storm in the late 1620s he made a vow that if he reached the harbour safely he would sell both his ship and its cargo and spend the money to benefit the poor. The Quirke Alms Houses stand to this day in Market House Lane bearing a plaque recording the event and the date 1630 when the houses were opened. There are also memorials to the Quirke family in the church.

Apart from access from the sea Minehead was not an easy place to reach and between 1705 and 1783 there was a decline in population, but in 1794 a directory noted that 'a number of persons of fashion have been induced to visit it as a bathing place'. After this the tourist industry began to benefit Minehead although as early as 1724 Daniel Defoe had written in *A Tour through England and Wales* that here was ... 'the best port and safest harbour, in all these counties ... No ship is so big, but it may come in, and no weather so bad, but the ships are safe when they are in ... The trade of this town lies chiefly with Ireland ... sends two members to Parliament ... The town is well built.'

After the railway reached Watchet from Taunton in 1862 a regular shuttle of coaches fed Minehead. On July 16th 1874 the railway reached Minehead and the resort was ready for take-off. Mary East celebrated the opening with a charming poem called 'The Local Line'.

'There are ten railway stations upon our little line;
First you come to Norton, and then there are nine.
Nine railway stations, and, if you are not late,
You come to Bishop's Lydeard and then there are eight.

Eight railway stations, with all their dawdling tricks,
You pass Crowcombe and Stogumber, and then there are six.
Six railway stations, and, if you but survive,
You come at last to Williton and then there are five.

Five railway stations; oh would there were no more
But you crawl along to Watchet, and then there are four.
And now you're going downhill, and bustle on quite fast,
And Washford and Blue Anchor are very quickly passed.

And then you come to Dunster, and gaze upon the sea
And when you reach dear Minehead how joyful you will be
As you gather up your luggage and hasten home to tea
And rest in peaceful Minehead, beside the whispering sea.'

The rail-link was a blessing to Minehead and on Whit Monday 1875 1,800 people came in by train. Fortunately after a short period of closure in the 1960s the West Somerset Line and all its ten stations have survived and a daily service is maintained, operating between April and October by both diesel and steam locomotives. The trains and the stations have been restored in the colours of the Great Western Railway and the 20 miles of track makes the West Somerset the longest privately-owned railway in Britain. Along the route are several museums and exhibitions including one concerned with the Great Western Railway at Blue Anchor and Washford and a permanent way exhibition at Crowcombe. Because this is an evolving railway we always prefer to start at Minehead Station and use the line as a base from which to explore Dunster, Blue Anchor, Watchet, Williton, Stogumber, Crowcombe and Bishops Lydeard. It is possible to break the journey at any point and there is a splendid

Selworthy Church can be seen clearly on the hillside from the A39.

Cistercian abbey at Cleeve between Blue Anchor and Watchet which should not be missed.

The Victorians liked nothing better than a bracing sea trip and the Bristol Channel was a popular place from which to enjoy views of Wales and on a nice day Minehead pier was a hive of activity. Once more tradition has been maintained in this area and the white funnel steamers are maintained by the Paddle Steamer Preservation Society which runs the paddle steamer 'Waverley' and the motor cruiser 'Balmoral'. On occasions, which are well-advertised, it is possible to visit Lundy and Steep Holme, although both vessels also operate from other resorts notably Ilfracombe and Bideford, as previously mentioned.

Another occasional transport gem which operates from Minehead is of even older vintage and take us back to the turnpike days. A horse-drawn mail coach has been restored to all its old glory, renamed 'The Lorna Doone' and a few lucky passengers can travel the old road route into Exmoor. This sort of treat can only be discovered by visitors who do their homework and consult the local Tourist Information Offices. The West Somerset Tourism Association is one of the few privately run associations of its kind left in the country. The officers and members of committees all give freely of their time and are pleased to help visitors enjoy the district which they themselves love so much. Their address is:

The West Somerset Tourism Association, The Town Hall, The Parade, Minehead, Somerset, TA24 5NB. Tel. 0643 702642.

Whilst Minehead is a seaside town for the historian its mild climate and nearby holiday camp ensure that it is well able to satisfy those in search of family fun be it with bucket and spade, on the back of a donkey, on the end of a fishing rod, tennis racket or golf club, pulling on a bow to dispatch an arrow or just sitting in the sun surrounded by the flowers in Blenheim Gardens. A recent innovation is Somerwest World on the seafront, an indoor extravaganza run by Butlins and which admits day visitors, between May and October. On offer are oasis fun pools, a sun-splash funfair, cable car and a mono-rail. There is also a boating lake and a roller-skating rink.

Each Sunday in summer there is a brass band concert in Blenheim Gardens and there are several festivals held, among which are the July Minehead and Exmoor Festival whilst in July and August there is the Minehead Carnival fortnight. In September the West Somerset Railway holds its gala week and anyone with a love of Victorian England and railways in particular should make tracks for Minehead at this time.

We read a tourist brochure before we visited Dunster and wondered if it was indeed one of 'Britain's gems'. We arrived in a snow storm and with a biting wind driving down its main street. Despite this we were not disappointed and when we returned in the summer we were convinced that even a tourist brochure could be guilty of understatement.!

The village is dominated, but in a friendly way, by a mighty castle which has been the focal point of the Minehead area since Norman times. The hill on which the castle stands once overlooked the sea and Dunster was a port but the tide's influence receded long ago. When the Normans arrived they found the Saxons had a hill fort on the hill, but the area was far too valuable not to be coveted by the followers of William of Normandy and the area was given to William de Mohun. This family held Dunster until 1376 when it was sold to Lady Elizabeth Luttrel and her descendants remained at Dunster until the castle was handed over to the National Trust. What is now called the Luttrel Arms was once called the Ship Inn, a reminder of when Dunster Haven

Selworthy is a delightful village now kept in wonderful condition by the National Trust.

was a port and the building belonged to the Abbot of Cleeve. During the Civil Wars of the 1640s Dunster was the scene of a bitter siege and the Parliamentarians caused great damage. No doubt the Luttrells fought a long battle of their own against decay and in the 19th century they extensively restored the building and produced an elegant country house. The gardens are a particular joy and contain many rare shrubs and trees. The views over the sea and to the Quantocks and Exmoor are as magnificent as they are panoramic. The castle and the grounds are open from Easter to the end of October. There is ample parking alongside the castle reached by a drive off the A39 rather than from the village centre. The old castle stable block has been converted into a comprehensively-stocked shop.

In addition to the castle there are many other attractions in Dunster which is one of the finest examples of a large medieval village, large enough, most people would say, to merit the status of a town.

We have made several visits to Dunster just to produce this chapter as there were so many features to photograph that we were spoilt for choice. What should take preference – the Water Mill, the Yarn Market or St George's Church. Then there was the Gallox packhorse bridge remaining much the same as in medieval times. There is also an excellent doll's museum and something which no book can ever successfully convey – the smell of the place. On a warm day Dunster is its own pot-pourri with roses,

Allerford is one of the finest packhorse bridges to be found in the West Country.

sandalwood and lavender wafting from the colourful gardens into the narrow alleys.

Dunster Mill is set on the River Avill and is a rare example of a corn mill being driven not by one wheel but by two. It is open from April until October and there is also an informative museum of agricultural machinery. Visitors can climb around the various levels of the mill which has been expertly restored to full working order and we can vouch for the excellence of the homemade bread which we made from the stoneground flour purchased from the mill. In 1884 Richard Jefferies visited the place and wrote that here was 'a curious mill which has two wheels overshot, both driven by the same sluice ... the mill dust sprinkled the foliage so that the leaves seemed scarce able to breathe; it dipped almost to the stream where trout were watching under a cloud of midges dancing over the ripples'. Few naturalists wrote as well as Jefferies but Dunster would inspire anyone to open their heart more than usual. Thomas Hardy wrote *A Laodicean* based on Dunster which he called Markton and he also changed the Luttrell's name to de Stancy. He set several scenes in Dunster's magnificent church.

As one would expect Dunster has a long ecclesiastical history and the Luttrell Arms originally belonged to the Abbot of Cleeve and the porch reflects this origin. It is probable that the slated building at the south end of the High Street was a monastic guest house for a priory which from the 12th to the 16th century existed just to the north of the church which it shared with the laity.

St George's itself dates mainly from the 15th and 16th centuries constructed in the Perpendicular style. There is no finer church in the area, but in Dunster it tends to be underrated because of the presence of the castle. The two should be visited as a matching couple as the Luttrell monuments are situated in the church, the best being dedicated to Elizabeth Luttrell depicted in alabaster and shown lying on an embroidered cushion. Other features of interest are the magnificent waggon roof dating from around 1500 and a rood screen which is said to be the longest in England.

One link with the past which has been all but lost can be seen by looking at a small sloping-topped desk with a substantial brass lock used by the Benedictine monks of Dunster Priory. The area which was once the abbey cloister is now a paved garden leading to a dovecote. This was used by the Benedictines to ensure a regular supply of young pigeons, called squabs. Pigeons breed throughout the year producing several clutches of two eggs. Many great houses and abbeys constructed pigeon houses, often round and containing niches in which the birds nested. They were encouraged to stay by being fed and with careful farming a regular supply of protein could be guaranteed. The Benedictines' dovecote has a remarkable revolving ladder which gave the brethren easy access to the nesting chambers.

In addition to being efficient farmers and provisioners the monks were also good businessmen who knew the value of a good communication system along which to carry their goods. Within the context of their time the packhorse bridges were as much a revolution as an inter-city train in modern times. Disbelievers should stand on Gallox Bridge on Park Street, Dunster at times of flood and imagine they were on their way to sell wares at the priory. Without the bridge a long detour would have been necessary or else an expensive wait for the waters to subside. The monks often charged a toll which they called a 'pontage' and which was used to keep the structures in good repair.

With a casual glance from a distance it appears that Dunster has not one castle but two. Conygarth Hill derives its name from Coney which was the Norman word for a rabbit. It was the

Dunster is one of Britain's most visited villages, with its famous Yarn Market and castle.

Normans who introduced the rabbit into England around 1100 and initially they were much valued for both their flesh and fur. They were kept in warrens usually on the top of rocky outcrops from which they could not burrow to escape. By 1776 the warren was no longer in use – rabbits were becoming so common as to be a nuisance – and the Luttrells decided to build a tower on Conygarth. They employed Richard Phelps, an artist born at Porlock, to design the tower and the household accounts for the castle indicate that a massive sum of £54 was paid for the workmen's cider. It is a wonder the tower stands straight!

A much more functional structure dominates the main street and Dunster's yarn market is arguably its most photographed feature. The building dates from about 1589 when an important cloth trade was being developed. The yarn needed by the weavers to make their broad cloths called 'Dunsters' which were mainly exported, came along the packhorse trails from all over Exmoor. Some wool was also spun by the occupants of the poor house in exchange for their food. The weavers made use of the nearby Grabbist Hill as 'tenter fields' where the cloth was pegged out to dry. The cloth was supported on hooks known as 'tenter-hooks' from which the modern saying derives. The hill has been owned by the National Trust since 1977.

Dunster is also the home of one of the finest doll museums in the country based on a collection originally made by Mrs Harwich.

There are dolls from Germany and France as well as Britain but the pride of the collection is one found in an Egyptian tomb. This just goes to prove that Dunster has a touch of everything with the added advantage that all these splendid sights are close together. A short walk leads to the restored railway station and the beach, for which a parking fee is charged. The beach is an attractive mix of sand, pebble and shingle.

Dunster can also be used as a base from which to explore a number of villages straddling the Brendon Hills.

CHAPTER 10

Villages around the Brendon Hills

The border of Exmoor is dotted with a number of small villages connected by narrow roads bordered by high hedges. There was some industry hereabouts but almost all the signs of this has gone giving the impression of quiet backwaters of thatch, bridges and tiny churches. Tourists can find the occasional excellent little inn, but most stay at Minehead, Taunton or perhaps at Watchet.

Withycombe, signposted off the A39 just beyond Dunster, is an almost hidden village with its church on a hill, at the bottom of which is a ford, whilst a road swinging away from the ford leads to Rodhuish, another secluded village. We once drove across the ford in search of a place to park to visit the church and when we got out of the car steam was issuing from the brakes which had worked so hard on the steep road to Withycombe. All there is here is a tangle of attractive cottages with orange-tiled roofs and the odd thatch plus the church dedicated to St Nicholas, but who could ask for more?

The church is painted white and almost hidden from the road by an ancient yew tree. This inspired the artist John William North, who lived in the village from 1904 to 1914, to paint The Old Yew Tree and Withycombe Church, the latter now in the Bristol Art Gallery. The church itself is mainly 13th century and has to a large extent been left alone. There is a rood screen carved by the same craftsmen who made such a fine job in Dunster church. There are also two interesting old effigies and a much more modern one.

The lid of a stone coffin on a windowsill in the north wall depicts a lady and although it is somewhat worn it does show a lacy head-dress. The second, that of a man, is more difficult to find and is set into a recess in the south wall and almost obscured by benches. Its suggested origins are equally obscure since it has been suggested that it represents Reginald Fitzurse who in 1169 was one of the murderers of Thomas à Becket. Most historians now agree, however, that this effigy is at least a century later than this tragic event.

The third effigy, if such it can be called, is modern and is the parishioners' celebration of their patron saint. This seems to us an excellent idea especially as we have walked round many churches all over Britain and have wanted to know more about the saint to whom the church is dedicated. We all know that St Nicholas is the Father Christmas we all love but who and what else was he? A label on the statue, which is illuminated for a fixed period at the press of a button, tells his story. St Nicholas was the 4th century Bishop of Myra in Asia Minor but his popularity really began in the east in the 9th century and in the west by the 11th century, perhaps brought back by the Knights from the Crusades. St Nicholas is known as the patron saint of sailors, merchants, and pawnbrokers, but especially of children. Such a popular man was bound to have a commercial value and in 1087 a group of Italian merchants stole his remains from Myra and enshrined them at Bari in Apulia. He is often known today as St Nicholas of Bari, but he did all his good works close to home at Myra. Some of his actions show that he followed the life and teachings of Christ and is said to have saved three girls from prostitution by paying their dowries of three bars of gold to enable them to marry well. He is also said to have helped many merchants and sailors who had fallen on hard times. How he was transferred from doing good in the hot deserts of Bari to a toy factory in Lapland is a product of the ever-fruitful European mind.

Withycombe Church has been given a liberal dose of white magic, but it also has a reminder of the blacker side of life as recorded by a brass tablet in the vestry. It tells the story of Joan Carne who is said to have died on 29 October 1612. It was said locally that at her house at Sandhill under the brooding Croydon Hill she had bewitched and killed three husbands. Proof, however, was lacking and she was given a proper Christian burial but when the mourners returned to her house she reappeared and cooked a meal. Perhaps this is no more unusual than transferring St Nicholas to Lapland!

Another reminder of a grim past is found just beyond the little hamlet of Rodhuish where there is a crossroads known as Felon's Oak. Obviously this was an ideal spot to site the gibbet on which rough justice was handed out to highwaymen and other evil-doers. We first visited the spot on a misty autumn evening with a slender half-crescent moon peeping through. The Felon's Oak

Comberow at the foot of the incline up Brendon Hill. Although the railway has now closed the incline can still be seen.

looked evil. Our next visit was on an April morning with the warm sun reflecting from the shiny petals of celandine and the gentle yellow of banks of primroses. The Felon's Oak looked friendly. The weather can certainly set the mood.

Opposite the oak are the gates of Croydon Hall, now a special school for maladjusted youngsters but it was at one time the home of Count Conrad von Hochberg, a German with a great love of England. What happened to the count would make an ideal plot for a novel along the lines of John Buchan's Richard Hannay stories. The count disappeared suddenly and without trace but in most mysterious circumstances just before the First World War.

Roadwater is much more modern than other villages but there are quiet places here among the traces of old and long-closed industries. Nearby at Cleeve are the considerable remains of the only Cistercian abbey in Somerset.

In the 19th century this was mining country and must have attracted the Knights of Exmoor who, as we have seen in Chapter 8, made their fortunes from iron. In 1839 mining was going on at Lethbridge, Chargot, Goosemoor, Withiel Hill and around Ralegh's Cross. In 1853 a group of Ironmasters based around Ebbw Vale set up the Brendon Hills Iron Ore Company, and opened their office at Watchet, an ideal port for connecting with Wales. Horse and cart transport was obviously far too slow and in July 1855 the West Somerset Mineral Railway Act was passed. Thirteen miles of track were planned from Watchet Harbour to Roadwater and then up to Brendon Hill – a difficult exercise in construction – and on to Heath Poult Cross. There was a branch to run from Brendon Hill to the mines of Ralegh's Cross.

The Watchet to Roadwater section was open for ore and passengers by April 1857 with platforms at Watchet, Washford and Roadwater which was then the vital connecting point for the ore. At the end of 1857 the line had been extended to Comberow at the foot of Brendon Hill and from which the engineers could look up, and contemplate the most difficult task – an incline of almost a mile in length with a gradient of 1 in 4 with ore waggons to be transported up and down by winding gear installed in an engine room at the top. By 1860 the track was complete, iron ore poured into Watchet and some villages on Exmoor were brought into the modern world within one hour of the line opening.

After an initial euphoria the iron-ore industry on Exmoor did not continue and cheaper Spanish ore undercut their prices and by 1883, the mines closed. Despite being deprived of the main bulk of its income, the railway continued for another few years, with passengers carried until 1898. An Australian-based company leased part of the line in 1911 to experiment with a new method of train control, but the rolling stock and even the rails were removed at the time of the First World War. Roadwater Station is now a private house and other parts of the track can still be recognised as part of Exmoor's industrial history.

A fine reminder of the ecclesiastical history of the area is Cleeve Abbey just beyond Roadwater on the road to Watchet. Now administered by English Heritage, the abbey is open throughout the year and has a good parking area. We have been lucky enough to visit Cleeve in every season and at various times of the day but it is at its best on a late spring morning with the sun reflecting from its pink-coloured sandstone. Although it is described as a ruin, compared to many of the larger Cistercian abbeys, especially in the north of England, Cleeve is remarkably substantial. The gatehouse and many of the domestic buildings remain in surprisingly good order, although the authorities have had to work hard on the ruins of the church in order to lay out its ground plan. Even in the depths of winter daisies and dandelions grow on the lawns and beside the Roadwater stream, which powered the abbey mill which still stands. No wonder the monks called their abbey 'Vallis Floridae' – the valley of flowers. In spring primroses, violets, stitchwort and speedwell grow everywhere and the local cottages on the roadside contribute their bit by growing dahlias, fuchsias, wallflowers and especially roses which scent the area from June until well into autumn. One cottage in particular deserves special attention as it marks the site of an ancient chapel dedicated to St Pancras. Virtually nothing of the chapel remains except a rather attractive lancet window but in the garden the holy well which once attracted pilgrims from far afield still exists.

Cleeve was established around 1190 as a daughter house of Revesby Abbey in Lincolnshire which was itself built in 1142. The land was given by William Earl of Roumare, and during the 13th century the abbey lived up to its monastic name and bloomed. The 14th century was one of some decline and although it revived again in the 15th century it was never one of the dominant English houses such as Tintern, Fountains or Furness which were set in fine farming country. Life around Exmoor was much tougher and communications cannot have been easy. Although the church has gone apart from a few low walls, in a historical sense this does not matter as we know that Cistercian churches were all built to a similar plan. The buildings around the cloisters are, however, almost complete and it is easy to get an accurate idea of how such an abbey was organised. The east range is 13th century and here is the well-preserved dorter or dormitory with stairs leading down towards the church, an ideal arrangement for the early services which were held to welcome the dawn of another day.

The redevelopment of the south range reflects the increased prosperity of the 15th century including the frater or dining room which still has its magnificent timbered roof. The dorter and the refectory are also sufficiently intact to reveal wall paintings dating from the 13th and 15th centuries. This gives a picture of Cistercian abbeys not as cold austere hunks of stone but with smooth interior walls illuminated by colourful biblical scenes.

The final view of Cleeve is of the gatehouse built in the 13th century but remodelled in the 16th and which also is complete enough to have a timbered roof. Originally it had two storeys and also served as the almonry where food was given to the poor. Above the archway is a Latin inscription which when translated reads 'Gate be open, shut to no honest person.' Although dissolved by Henry VIII, in 1536, along with many other small abbeys, Cleeve still remains a tranquil spot with a friendly atmosphere emanating from its walls.

Another village with religious connections is Monksilver which had links with Goldcliffe Priory across the Bristol Channel in the old Welsh county of Monmouthshire. Despite all these references to gold and silver plus the mines around Roadwater suggesting a mining connection, the word silver is thought to derive from the twisting little stream which meanders its way to meet the sea at Doniford. It may also derive from sylvan, meaning 'in the woods'. There is certainly iron in the soil, however, and its rusty red colour contrasts delightfully with the lush green fields which can only ever be produced in areas of high rainfall. The village itself is a splendid mixture of colour with the Notley Arms and a

19th-century barn now converted into Half Moon Cottage, a private dwelling house. Standing in an elevated position is All Saints Church, guides for which are on sale at both Half Moon Cottage and the Notley Arms and the latter also has a good wholesome range of bar snacks.

A remarkably refreshing feature of Exmoor is that almost all the churches are open at all times and All Saints at Monksilver is no exception. The first rector was Thomas de Combe in 1324, but it is more than likely that there was a church, and perhaps a preaching cross, long before this. After being governed by the Welsh monks until the Reformation the living was given to the deans and canons of Windsor in order to benefit education. Thus Monksilver coffers were likely to have been used to benefit Eton School which was initially run from Windsor. Prior to rectors the church may have had a vicar, who was originally defined as someone who took a service vicariously, in other words on behalf of someone else. The rector by contrast was much more in charge of his own destiny and that of the parish. Further evidence of an early church can be seen by looking at the base of the tower which looks 13th century. The gargoyles are also ancient and grotesque even if they are worn by time. There are similar ugly figures on Wells Cathedral and we wonder if Button, the 13th-century Bishop of Bath and Wells, may not have been the inspiration. After all he was said to be the patron saint of toothache!

There is much to admire inside All Saints, especially the carved bench ends depicting fish, a fine stag and the Green Man, an unconscious reminder perhaps of long forgotten paganism. There is also an eagle lectern, one of only two in the whole of the county of Somerset. In the sanctuary area is a fine piscina and a very rare example of an altar of repose, also known as an Easter sepulchre, which is still in use. There is a well-worked screen and a rood stairway leading up to the roof, although the doorway which once allowed access onto the screen has long been blocked up. There is also a 16th-century pulpit which is now entered through a hole in the wall. The waggon roof is a treasure dating perhaps from the 13th century, yet another piece of evidence to suggest that the church was in existence prior to the arrival of the first rector.

Close to the door is an old alms box bearing the inscription

'Bee merciful after thy power, thee that hath pitie upon the poore lendeth unto the Lord'.

In the churchyard is another ancient yew and also the famous murder tombstone. Beneath this lie old Mrs Elizabeth Conibrer and her two daughters found murdered in the nearby hamlet of Woodford. The inscription shows no sign of turning the other cheek and the words aimed at the brutal killer read 'Inhuman Wretch! Where'er thou Art -'. The unfinished epithet speaks volumes.

Other more pleasant gravestones are in memory of the Notley family who once owned Combe Sydenham on the outskirts of Monksilver on the way to Elworthy. Later the manor passed into the hands of the Sydenham family. It was in 1580 that Sir George Sydenham erected the present building on a more ancient foundation, his construction having four towers. Three of these towers and one complete wing of the house were destroyed during the Civil War, but it was rebuilt after the Restoration of Charles II in 1660.

Few houses are approached after passing road signs reading 'Beware of the Peacocks' but the warnings are real enough. The single remaining tower is surrounded by a jig-saw of red walls and roofs and during the summer the house and gardens are open to the public. There is a lunch and tea room, gift shop, woodland walks, an Elizabethan herb garden and a working fish farm from which trout can be purchased. There is a large car park. Combe Sydenham has close associations with Sir Francis Drake and with Richard Jefferies. It is said that Elizabeth Sydenham, heiress of the manor, became engaged to Drake who then set off on one of his long voyages. Thinking herself deserted Elizabeth became engaged to marry another at Stogumber. Just as the ceremony was starting Drake is said to have fired a cannon ball from 'across the world' which landed on her train and sent the terrified lass scurrying home to await the return of Sir Francis. He had returned by 1585 (three years before the Armada) and Elizabeth became his second wife. But what of the cannon ball which spent some time at Taunton Museum before being returned to Combe Sydenham where it is now on display? It is more than likely to be a meteorite, but the story is well worth the telling.

As we walked round the estate we could see that little had changed since Richard Jefferies wrote about it in 1880. Between our two visits we had read his account of Monksilver and Combe Sydenham, the latter described in a chapter of his book *Red Deer* which is headed 'A Manor House in Deer Land'.

The church at Elworthy has not fared so well as others in and around Exmoor. It is now officially declared redundant, but fortunately this does not mean that it will be allowed to decay. As is the case at Parracombe the fabric is maintained by the efforts of the Redundant Churches Fund based at St Andrews-by-the-Wardrobe in Queen Victoria Street, London. During 1991 St Martin's Church was repaired and the 13th-century building is now safe. Although a small church – the congregation was never large – there is a lovely old screen bearing the inscription 'Lord Prepare our Arts to pray, Anno- 1632'.

The Elworthy area was settled long before Christian times and at nearby Willet, a grass-covered mound was excavated in 1834 to reveal bones and artefacts which have been ascribed to the Bronze Age. Also found were barley grains and the impression of a potter's board in clay.

The name Elworthy is Saxon and almost certainly means Ella's clearing. Perhaps the Saxons merely took over the hill fort of Iron-age settlers who constructed an impressive defensive earthworks called Elworthy Barrows, situated about a mile to the south-west of the modern hamlet at a height of 1200 feet (365.6m).

It is worth the effort to visit the fort, now snug beneath a blanket of varied vegetation, not only for the view from the summit but also to search for an ancient highway. This was probably used in turn by Bronze-age people then as an Iron-age track taken over in turn by Roman, Saxon, monk-traders and finally by packhorse trains winding around the Brendon Hills.

Many of these old routes meet at Ralegh's Cross which even today is nothing more than an attractive inn surrounded by lawns and a children's play area. But stop awhile and look around you. Here is a mounted board recording that this was a beacon site long before the Armada. At one time there were two beacons kept in constant readiness – one was to be lit as a warning, two in the case of a dire emergency. The fires were in direct line with those on Cleeve Hill overlooking Watchet from whence a seaborne landing was most likely to come. On the inland side the Ralegh fire would be seen from the heights of Dunkery Beacon and from here all Exmoor could be alerted. The still prominent fire points have not been essential since the Napoleonic Wars but almost hidden behind a mound of grass is a pill-box which is to be preserved as a reminder of the defensive preparations of the Second World War.

Between Ralegh's Cross and the A39 road is the delightful little settlement of Withiel Florey but if you are exploring by car do not blink or you will miss a real treasure. There is a small parking area on a sharp bend in the road at Castle Hill Farm and overlooking this is a charming little white church, built of Brendon Hill stone and roofed with Treborough slate.

Immediately on entering the little church we were greeted by the smell of paraffin issuing from the lamps hanging from the roof. There are no mod cons here, only good old Victorian reminders with a blow-organ, its music stand lit by candles. The church is often full of fresh flowers or when these are out of season displays of dry vegetation, including teasels which were once scraped across cloth to raise the nap and improve its appearance and qualities of insulation.

Teasels are grown commercially in many parts of Somerset both for local use and for export to northern mills. They are also used in the manufacture of felt for snooker and pool tables. Teasels are biennial plants so they are grown on a two-year cycle. They are sown in March but the seeds take time to germinate and they need to be kept free of competing weeds throughout the summer. They are transplanted in October using land which has been ploughed following straw cutting. In the transplanting process a special spade called a 'splitter' is used with an edge to cut through the very long tap root. The following July the plants flower and are ready for harvesting in August. The heads are cut by hand with the workers wearing gloves and using small sharp knives which are crescent shaped. They are then dried in the open for around three weeks before being taken into barns for storage prior to selling.

When the West Country was a centre for weaving especially around Dunster the teasels were a vital crop. It is good to see it surviving even though the demand for natural material is slackening as technology comes up with ever more alternatives.

On the way from Ralegh's Cross to Withiel Florey the road passes close to the once famous incline of the West Somerset

The gatehouse of the Cistercian abbey at Cleeve is one of the finest pieces of monastic architecture surviving in Britain.

Mineral Railway, the line twisting around the little hamlet and then on to Gupworthy which was the terminus of the line. The station house still stands and for those with plenty of time to enjoy an exploratory walk, armed with an ordnance survey map, it is possible to find broken bridges festooned with ferns, bramble and herb Robert and also a number of long-sealed entrances to iron mines, themselves surrounded by more than a century's greenery.

Whilst Gupworthy and Withiel Florey are off the beaten track, Wheddon Cross lies astride the relatively major road, the A396 between Dunster and Dulverton. The crossroads houses the modern settlement but the Church of St John is situated along a narrow side road at Cutcombe. The meeting of so many roads was an ideal place for a sheep fair and early autumn from the Middle

Ages onwards Cutcombe Sheep Fair has been a feature of Exmoor life. Wheddon Cross is on the highest ridge between Dulverton and Dunster and overlooks the valleys of the River Avill which flows northwards to the sea and the Quarme which flows in the opposite direction to its junction with the Exe at Coppleham Cross. This has long been walking country for tourists and in the later years of the 18th century Coleridge and the Wordsworths wandered these lanes. Folk from Lakeland do not see William as a controversial figure but he was not made very welcome in Devon and Somerset as he was well known for his avowed sympathies with the French revolutionaries. From Wheddon Cross the modern visitor can walk via Cutcombe to Timberscombe and explore the red sandstone church dedicated to the Celtic Petrock. From the church a rough track leads to the now deserted village of Clicket and another delightful stroll, especially in February, leads to snowdrop valley. All streamlets hereabouts find their way into the Avill river which is spawned high on Dunkery Hill which can be reached by returning to Wheddon Cross crossing the main road and heading towards Porlock.

On a clear day, whatever the season, the views from the highest point on Exmoor are breathtaking and a good number of car parks have been provided from which walks of less than a mile snake up to the famous beacon. The beacon stands 1704 feet (519 m) above sea level and was described in fiction by Blackmore who suggested that the Doones used to light the fire when on their way home from plundering the Exmoor villages. In fact there have probably been fire hearths here since the Bronze Age and all must have been in readiness when the Saxons fought the Danes and when, as at Ralegh's Cross, the beacons were manned when the Armada was expected and at the time of the Napoleonic wars. When Wordsworth was exploring the area Napoleon was on the rampage and local folk may well have thought he was a spy.

There are staggeringly beautiful views towards Dartmoor, over the Bristol Channel to Wales and down to the sea at Watchet. It has been said that seventeen counties of old England can be seen from the Dunkery. Our problem, however, is to lift our eyes from the ground as this is naturalists' country. To the untrained eye the soaring buzzard seems eagle-like as it scans the moor, a habitat it shares with the merlin. Mammals often seen here include fox, badger, stoat and weasel. Botanists too are excited when they find round-leaved sundew and butterwort, both of which can supplement the minerals which are in short supply here, by trapping and digesting insects. Among the stands of heather adders occur and common lizards are exactly that; whortleberries are still gathered but the cranberry for some reason has become somewhat rare. For those who arrive early and stay late the folds of Dunkery Hill provide frequent sightings of red fox and also deer. The climb from Wheddon Cross reveals open country but the steep and narrow descent on the Porlock side discloses belts of trees, both alien conifers and native oak and birch. There are any number of secluded parking places ideal for picnics on days when the exposed places are too chilly.

Those who enjoy walking rather than driving should set aside a day here. Park close to the marked nature trail and follow Horner Water down towards West Luccombe, passing two little packhorse bridges on the way. It is best to return to the car park via Luccombe, an exquisitely unspoiled village of thatch, coloured sandstone walls and fragrant gardens. All this would be enough but there is also the 13th-century church of St Mary with fragments of medieval stained glass thoughtfully removed from Selworthy during a typically brash spate of early Victorian restoration in 1840.

On the north wall is a story which would provide Blackmore with the basis of another novel if we could but raise him from the dead. Told in coloured glass is the story of a cleric active on the side of the king during the Civil War. Dr Henry Byam was vicar of both Selworthy and Luccombe and he was so outspoken in support of Charles I that the Parliamentarian soldiers thought it advisable to arrest him. His wife and daughter managed to escape along with the household servants but they were tragically drowned whilst attempting to cross the Bristol Channel. Byam with his sons was resourceful enough to escape and joined the king. Following the execution of Charles in January 1649 Byam escaped once more with the young King Charles II and the vicar spent his time until the monarchy was restored in 1660 on the Scilly Isles. He was then restored to his parish at Luccombe dying there in 1669 at the grand old age of 89. Folks must be afraid to die at Luccombe because paradise may not be quite so pretty! It is at its best in spring when the village hedgerows opposite an attractive little stream are a mass of primrose and lesser celandine.

Those who do not worry about driving along narrow roads with steep drops will be rewarded with the sight of the two isolated villages of Cloutsham and Stoke Pero. Cloutsham consists of a solidly attractive farm which offers a holiday cottage to let and from which a network of footpaths lead to National Trust woodlands. The most scenically rewarding lead in one direction to Horner and in the other towards Dunkery Beacon.

Stoke Pero is a tiny hamlet and its 12th-century church is, at 1013 feet (309 metres), the highest church on Exmoor. The origins of the hamlet are not precisely known but there was a local family of Norman descent named Piro. Only the tower and the porch are original having been retained during the 1897 restoration, but the interior is lit by candles and the organ is operated by a pump. The church has no patron saint but has a happy feel to it.

From Luccombe and from the car park below Dunkery Beacon it is a short way back to the A39 and the completion of this necklace of Exmoor villages. Now it is time to turn to Watchet, the major port of the area.

CHAPTER 11

Around Watchet – Exmoor's Working Harbour

Although it lies just outside the boundaries of the National Park, no account of Exmoor would be complete without reference to its major port which opens out into the Severn Sea and has achieved a remarkable double – catering for industry and for tourists. The old track of the Mineral Railway ended at the harbour and now forms a fascinating walk and another day can be spent around the harbour itself which has been tastefully pedestrianised. Over a thousand years of Watchet's history has been crammed into the Market House Museum overlooking the harbour; it is open at Easter and then from mid-May to the end of September. The times of opening are daily from 10.30 am to 12.30 pm and from 2.30 pm to 4.30 pm but during July and August it also opens between 7 pm and 9 pm. The entry fee is nominal and there is some parking plus a sales point and audio-visual displays dealing with local history. Some effort is made to cater for the disabled but the entrance steps are rather difficult to manoeuvre. There are many historic photographs of the harbour, the surrounding area and old sailing vessels plus figureheads. Paintings and models are all laid out as only enthusiastic amateurs can do. There are no stuffy curators here and those who want to know anything and have time to listen need only ask.

The best way to understand the origins and development of Watchet is to stand on Cleeve Hill to the west of the town when it can be seen that the settlement nestles at the mouth of a narrow valley. This fulfils every one of the factors needed to establish a small port. Bronze- and Iron-Age settlements were plentiful in the area and doubtless the sheltered bays and estuaries would have been ideal for fishing and the gathering of shellfish.

Burrough, the Victorian historian, suggested that the word Somerset derived from the old English *Seo-Mere – Saetan* which translates as 'dwellers by the sea lakes'. Celtic tribes existed in the Watchet area and the museum at Taunton has examples of dug-out canoes which in good weather would allow contact with their main settlements in South Wales. There are place names still in use which confirm the Celtic connections such as *Afon* meaning water, *Tun* or *Ton* meaning an enclosure, *Dun* signifying a hill-fort, *Tre* a dwelling place and Combe is a Saxon word derived from the Celtic *Cwm* meaning a valley. As we have seen throughout this book all the above words are in constant use on Exmoor.

There are several suggestions in current use to explain the name Watchet. One of the least probable in our view is that it is derived from *Waese,* meaning a land washed by water, which could refer to the tidal movements. Usually, however, it is best to refer to the work of Ekwall who suggests that Anglo-Saxon derivation means a settlement beneath a wood and this still fits Watchet to the present day. Despite the fact that the Romans knew the area it was not until Saxon times that Watchet developed and at this time it became one of the most important towns in south-western England. By the time Alfred the Great (AD 871 to 901) ruled the then kingdom of Wessex, Watchet was already established thanks to the efforts of Ecyberht, the West Saxon King, who in AD 815 pushed the Celts into Exmoor and after a period of fierce fighting chased them across the Severn Sea into Wales.

Also by Alfred's time an important Saxon mint had been set up at Watchet. Whilst this established Watchet as an important town, mints were more widely dispersed in Saxon England than in the present day and other Somerset towns engaged in coining were Axbridge, Bath, Bruton, Cadbury, Crewkerne, Ilchester, Langport, Milborne Port, Petherton and Taunton. The thorough researches of A. L. Wedlake traced Watchet coins in museum collections to the reigns of Aethelred (21 coins) Canute (12 coins) Harold (3 coins), Harthacnut (2 coins) and Edward the Confessor (5 coins). In addition to the king's image the coiner also had to impress his own name which enabled the king's officials to check the weight of the coin. The Watchet mint only produced silver pennies and the names of Sigeric Hunewine and Godcild indicate Watchet moneyers. Although no Watchet examples have been found it was customary for folk to cut the silver pennies in half to produce half-pennies and into quarters to produce farthings.

A study of the dispersal of coinage can tell historians a great deal about social and military events of a given period and

Watchet coins have turned up in museums in Scandinavia especially at Copenhagen in Denmark. They were obtained from hoards of treasure found at Jutland and Zealand and this means just one thing – Danegeld. This was paid by the Saxons to the Danes during the 10th and 11th centuries to prevent pillage, a very satisfactory arrangement for the latter and an acceptable compromise for the former. Not all Saxons submitted to such a tax and the good folk of Watchet did not easily part with their coinage. The Anglo-Saxon records show that in AD 918 the Danes attacked Watchet and Porlock but they 'were beaten on both occasions, so that few of them came away save only those who have swam out to the ships'. Florence of Worcester writing in the late 10th century described a more successful raid from the Dane's point of view, which took place in AD 977 when they 'entered the mouth of the River Severn, and ravaged sometimes Cornwall, sometimes North Wales, and then Watchet in Devonshire (as it then was) and there brought great evil in burning and man slaying.'

There were further attacks in AD 988 and 997, but Albany Major has suggested that the people of Watchet may, in between times at least, have conducted some peaceful trade with the Danes. Thus the coinage may have arrived in Scandinavia either as a result of trade, Danegeld or by outright plundering, but more than likely as a combination of the three.

Watchet is mentioned in the Domesday Survey of 1088 published some 22 years after the conquest and is listed as belonging to William de Moion, the first Norman holder of Dunster. Agriculturally Watchet was not important but it was significant as a trading centre and the mint continued in operation during the reigns of William I (1066-1087), William II (1087-1101) and Stephen (1135-1154).

Apart from its mint which declined gradually Watchet was important as an ecclesiastical centre, and gradually established itself as an industrial port which it has managed to retain to the present day, the decline in the iron industry being balanced by an increase in the manufacture of paper.

Watchet Church commands a fine view of the town and harbour, being one of the largest in the area and is dedicated to the Celtic St Decuman. It is said that he journeyed across the Severn Estuary from Wales in a flimsy coracle perhaps being

This jolly band of wassailers was photographed in 1931.

towed by a cow which also provided him with milk. He was said to have been attacked and decapitated but his head was restored by the healing waters of a holy well. It has been suggested that there may have been a church on this site from the 5th century, but it was probably just a preaching cross. From the present building, mainly 15th century but with some 13th-century parts, it is possible to see the contours of the Quantocks and the Brendons which dovetail into Exmoor, the two being separated by the valley of the River Quarme. The tower of the church is so battlemented that it would look more at home as the keep of a castle and it obviously had the dual function of protection and religion. Parts of the chancel are 13th century and the central passage floor is tiled and these are illustrated with shields and the coats of arms of Somerset families. It would seem likely that these were made at Cleeve Abbey which had a profitable business producing these tiles. Another connection with Cleeve Abbey concerns a bell made in Exeter by Robert Norton during the reign of Henry VI (1422-1461). This came to Watchet when the abbey was dissolved and hung in the tower around 1539. The bell is inscribed 'Est michi collatum istud nomen amatum' which translates as 'it is my duty to give forth that beloved name'.

There are many attractive church roofs in the area in and around Exmoor and St Decumans is no exception with its waggon structure dating from the 15th century; it has a number of finely carved bosses and at the base of the supportive braces there are carved angels holding scrolls bearing inscriptions of shields and books, whilst on the opposite side to the north of the church they are shown holding hammer, nails, rope and a cross. The screens are also excellent examples of the art of the woodcarver whilst the stone-mason's skills are shown to marvellous effect in a mural beneath the east window of the north chancel. Work of this type is very rare in Britain and this example shows John Windham, who died in 1645, and Mabel his wife who passed away 12 years before. The work was done by the well-named Nicholas Stone who was master mason to both James I and Charles I.

The Wyndhom (or Windham) family are also commemorated in the north chapel which contains some impressive monuments but it is mainly the brasses which delight the social historian. The best of an impressive collection are those of Sir John Windham, who died in 1574, and his wife Elizabeth who died in 1571. Sir John is shown in the armour of a knight of the period and his wife is wearing an impressive dress. Her hair is parted in the middle and covered by what became known as a French hood during the period when Mary Queen of Scots was in the news. The skirt is left delicately open to reveal an embroidered petticoat. There are also brasses of another John Windham who died in 1572 and his wife Florence who died in 1596, which combined with the first two make Watchet Church an ideal pilgrimage for students of Tudor fashion.

As far as industry is concerned Watchet was famous in the 15th century for limeburning and the Luttrells were good customers as extensions were made to their castle at Dunster. Whilst writing his book *A Tour through the Island of Great Britain,* published in 1724, Defoe found that 'On this coast are vast quantities of rock, or rather pebble which the sea at low water leaves uncovered from whence the neighbouring inhabitants fetch them on shore to an higher ground and burn them into lime, for dressing their land but it is more especially used in building, as no cement whatsoever is most lasting ... The cliffs are stored with alabaster, which by the wash of the sea, falls down and so conveyed from hence to Bristol ... Neither should it be omitted that the inhabitants burn great quantities of sea-weed to supply the glass makers of Bristol'.

Watchet alabaster seems to have been in great demand and in some cases was preferred to that from Derbyshire and Gerard, writing in 1633, pointed out that Watchet material was harder and had a greater variety of colours, including some pure white but also some black spotted with white as well as a reddish variety. The fact that Watchet was a port and the Derbyshire deposits were inland also made transportation easier and therefore cheaper. The inferior alabaster was ground up to produce gypsum and this was quarried from the cliffs between Watchet and Blue Anchor. It was shipped mainly to Bristol where it was used to make plaster of Paris and also in paper making which continued until 1914 although, as we shall see later, Watchet is still concerned with the paper industry.

The port also has a long association with fishing and so it is perhaps fitting that the harbour and the activity around it is said to have inspired Coleridge to write the poem 'The Ancient Mariner'. Wool and cloth were not exported from Watchet because Minehead was defined as the staple port and this compelled all traders to export via this harbour. The folk of Watchet, Tiverton and Taunton objected to such a monopoly but there was a reason which at the time would seem to have been logical. All exports were concentrated to just a few staple ports and the ships which sailed from them could be protected against pirates and the taxes due on the exports could be centrally collected.

As the 17th century drew to a close Watchet, along with many other areas of coastal England, was making a good profit from smuggling. In 1682 a report sent to Charles II noted that the people of Watchet 'from being beggars within this ten years the whole town has grown exceeding rich ... and it was found that several small vessels had no other business but that of running goods, and that the collector of customs there usually sat drinking with the masters of ships while gangs of men were unloading them', William Dashwood was the official on the make and although he was eventually suspended he had almost certainly made his fortune by then. The smugglers continued for some time longer and there is documentary evidence suggesting fairly frequent battles between the runners and the excise man.

Watchet harbour reached its peak of prosperity in the 1860s when coal was imported and the iron mines between the Brendons and Exmoor were at their most efficient. Tourism was also beginning and steamers from Bristol and South Wales unloaded tourists by the hundred.

In 1866 we get some idea of how far the Victorians would go in pursuit of fun. 'One of Dale's steamboat excursions brought 300 people from Bristol on Whit-Monday. Their landing caused some little amusement, for being too late to find water enough to enter the harbour, the passengers were brought ashore, some in boats, others in carts, and not a few on the backs of men. Some in their eagerness to get ashore were thoroughly drenched, others found themselves too deep in mud to be comfortable.' Richard Stoates Dale who died in Cardiff in 1899 was a good example of Victorian versatility, using his boats as tugs in the winter and converting them to pleasure steamers during the season. So popular were the latter that in the 1860s as many as three boats would leave Watchet for Ilfracombe each day.

Because of the increase in trade the harbour was redesigned in 1861, and in 1862 the railway arrived from Taunton both combining to stimulate trade and tourism. Dale's dual purpose boats were replaced by specially built pleasure steamers owned by the Red Funnel and White Funnel lines, the latter still operating in the Bristol Channel, but there is no longer a service out of Watchet which is a pity. Commercially the harbour of the 1860s handled coal, wheat, timber, flour, iron ore and paper with connections with the Bristol Channel ports, London, Liverpool and Ireland. By the end of the 19th century the iron ore trade had declined to nothing and Watchet Harbour was badly damaged by storms in the first few years of the 20th century. Flour milling which had been a feature of the town from Saxon times also declined but the relative prosperity of the labour was maintained by paper manufacture.

Watchet Paper Mills has an ancestry dating back to the Middle Ages, and many farmers supplemented their income by producing paper from wood pulp as a cottage industry. The large mill operating today was founded around 1750 by William Wood and passed through many hands but has remained on the same site, although it has expanded a great deal, and is now vital to both the port and as a direct employer of labour. Much of the paper goes to Spain and Portugal. In the 1990s paper and tourists spell Watchet.

Watchet also provides a good base from which to explore a number of villages including Blue Anchor, Carhampton, Washford and Williton. The road from Watchet to Blue Anchor is narrow, undulating and twisting but for those with time to spare there is a network of footpaths through woodlands and along the coastline. There is nothing at Blue Anchor apart from a splendid sandy beach but do not look inland for too long unless you like serried ranks of caravans.

The village of Carhampton is set on the A39 and it is easy to drive through it and miss a real gem of a church, although it is the interior which is so remarkable. Here is a rood screen which is not left as plain wood but is still brightly painted. We really enjoyed the feel that the religious furniture of pre-Reformation England was as colourful as in many Catholic countries today – a fact also apparent from a visit to Cleeve Abbey described in the last chapter. Another piece of Carhampton history which we discovered whilst passing through the village on January 15th was that in two days Wassail Night would be celebrated. This once widespread ancient custom is now only remembered in two Somerset villages – Norton Fitzwarren and here at Carhampton. What a night it turned out to be. Everyone drank cider, bread was toasted over a bonfire and dipped in cider, a band played, everybody sang, apples were roasted, all of which we could understand. But just why shot guns were fired into the branches was beyond us. Fortunately help was at hand, as the locals were only too pleased to explain the rituals of the custom, and to let us join in the toast to the Wassail Queen.

The apple crop is still important in these parts as it probably has been since pagan times when the actual trees were worshipped. Wassailing was a turning of the year thank you for the fruit and a plea for more of the same next year. It became entangled with the twelfth night celebrations in medieval England. When the calendar was adjusted in England round about 1750 twelfth night was celebrated on January 6th. The wassailers stuck to the 16th. Wassail means 'good health', but we still have the modern embellishment of the shot gun. This is to make sure that the trees are awake, appreciate the plea being made to them and answer it in the affirmative. No doubt chanting has always been part of the ceremony, but the modern words have been given Christian overtones. We cannot now pass through Carhampton without conjuring up the insistent rhythm of the wassailers' song.

'Old Apple Tree, Old Apple Tree
We wassail thee, and asking thee to bear,
For only Jesus knows where we shall be
Till Apples come another year.
Please thee bear well and also bloom well
So merry we can be
Let all take off their hats and doff them all to thee
Old Apple Tree, Old Apple Tree,
We wassail thee and ask you soon to bear
Hat-fulls
Cap-fulls
Three bushel bag-fulls
And some to store under the stacks!'

Next comes Washford, another point from which Cleeve Abbey can be visited and which we described in the last chapter. There is another treat here, however, set at the junction of the A39 and the B3190 to Watchet. Here is Tropicaria which is open from 10 am to 6 pm during March through to October but in the period November to February it only opens at weekends and during school holidays from 10 am to 4 pm. It is situated inside a converted BBC transmitting station but the tall radio masts have been retained and are visible for miles around. The complex looks more like a radar station than the fine tourist attraction which it is. There is ample free parking, an adventure playground, picnic area, cafeteria and a gift-shop. Inside has been created a tropical jungle and a section of rain forest plants, their branches at times seeming to overflow with free-flying tropical birds. There are spiders, toads, terrapins, lizards, iguanas and snakes. We watched children plucking up courage to touch some of the friendly snakes and it was amazing to see how quickly they relaxed when they realised that the reptiles were warm and dry and not all cold or slimy.

Downstairs there is a crypt brilliantly lit and housing a varied display of corals and catfish, lobsters and exotic fish. Outside in the gardens there are aviaries but there is also a display of fire engines and equipment which, although unexpected, is interesting and the children love it.

Just beyond Washford is Williton and just off Bridge Street is Orchard Mill, a 17th-century building in a very pretty setting. A museum is housed in the old mill built in 1616 and features agricultural implements plus an odd assortment of Victorian and Edwardian bric-a-brac. It is not often we have seen coopers' tools near an early vacuum cleaner or an almost prototype washing machine next to a plough. There are three storeys crammed with more than 1,000 exhibits. Outside, however, is the best exhibit of all, the huge overshot waterwheel which has been accurately restored.

The orchard garden allows time to reflect on the past and listen to the sound of water splashing on the wheel. Before following one of several footpaths up to villages with such charming names as Stream and Yarde few can resist an Orchard Mill cream tea even when breakfast is hardly digested! The restaurant here is actually very good and vegetarians are also catered for. The restaurant even opens in the evenings although reservations have to be made, and as there is no license guests are welcome to bring their own wine.

There is plenty of free parking and the mill is open daily except Monday from 1st March to 31st October and also on weekends during November and December. In the months of April and October the mill also closes on Tuesdays. For those on holiday the craft shop offers a wide range of locally made gifts which make lovely and unusual presents.

Whilst the places described in this chapter form an ideal basis for a car tour, they can also be visited by using the West Somerset Steam Railway from either Taunton or Minehead. They also provide a last lingering look at Exmoor before exploring Somerset, yet another beautiful and historic English county.

Further Reading

Allen, N.V. (1971) *The Birds of Exmoor* (The Exmoor Press)
Binding, Hilary (1983) *Old Minehead and Around* (The Exmoor Press)
Brown, C.A. (1964) *The Lynton and Barnstaple Railway* (David & Charles)
Burrows, R. (1971) *The Naturalist in Devon and Cornwall* (David & Charles)
Burton, S.H. (1975) *The Lorna Doone Trail* (The Exmoor Press)
Burton, S.H. (1984) *Exmoor* (Robert Hale)
Catchpole, C.T. (1972) *The Lynton and Barnstaple Railway* (The Oakwood Press)
David, Joy (1989) *The Hidden Places of Devon and Cornwall* (Maps Marketing)
Dent, A. (1970) *The Pure-bred Exmoor Pony* (Author)
Evered, P. (1902) *Staghunting on Exmoor* (Chatto and Windus)
Farr, Grahame (1970) *Ships and Harbours of Exmoor* (The Exmoor Press)
Fox, Lady Aileen, (1964) *South West England* (Thames & Hudson)
Freethy, Ron (1983) *The Naturalists' Guide to the British Coastline* (David & Charles)
Freethy, Ron (1986) *The Woodlands of Britain* (Bell & Hyman)
Giddens, Caroline J. (1980) *Minehead. A Little History* (Alcombe Books)
Goss, F. (1931) *Memories of a Stag Hunter* (Witherby)
Jefferies, Richard (1892) *Red Deer* (Longman)
Madge, Robin (1971) *Railways around Exmoor* (The Exmoor Press)
MacDermot, E.T. (1973) *A History of the Forest of Exmoor* (David & Charles) First published in 1911.
Miles, Roger (1972) *The Trees and Woods of Exmoor* (The Exmoor Press)
Patten, R.W. (1974) *Exmoor Custom and Song* (The Exmoor Press)

Peel, J.H.B. (1970) *Portrait of Exmoor* (Hale)
Rawle, E.J. (1903) *The Doones of Exmoor* (Barnicott & Pearce, Taunton 1903)
Sellick, R. (1962) *The West Somerset Mineral Railway* (David & Charles)
Snell, F.J. (1903) *A Book of Exmoor* (Methuen)
Speed, J.G. and Speed M.G. (1977) *The Exmoor Pony* (Countrywide Livestock)

Index